THE FUNNIEST JOKES IN THE WORLD

H.D. Shourie had a long career of some thirty-five years in government service, beginning with the civil service in pre-Partition Punjab. At the time of Independence, he was the City Magistrate of Lahore. immediately thereafter he held the post of Deputy Commissioner for Refugee Relief in Punjab for four years.

As part of the Indian Administrative Service, he was responsible for setting up the National Productivity Council and the Indian Institute of Foreign Trade. After retirement he was with the United Nations for three years.

About twenty years ago he set up the public interest organization Common Cause dedicated to consumer protection in India. He has been the Director of this organization since its inception.

H.D. Shourie is almost ninety and lives in New Delhi.

PENGUIN BOOKS

The
Funniest
Jokes
in the World

Compiled by
H D Shourie

PENGUIN BOOKS

Penguin Books India (P) Ltd., 11 Community Centre, Panchsheel Park,
New Delhi 110017, India
Penguin Books Ltd., 27 Wrights Lane, London W8 5TZ, UK
Penguin Putnam Inc., 375 Hudson Street, New York, NY 10014,
USA
Penguin Books Australia Ltd., Ringwood, Victoria, Australia
Penguin Books Canada Ltd., 10 Alcorn Avenue, Suite 300, Toronto,
Ontario M4V 3B2, Canada
Penguin Books (NZ) Ltd., Cnr Rosedale & Airborne Roads, Albany,
Auckland, New Zealand

First published by Penguin Books India 2001

Copyright ©Penguin Books India 2001

10 9 8 7 6 5 4 3 2 1

Typeset in Century Schoolbook by Wordkraft Editorial Services,
New Delhi

Printed at Chaman Offset Printers, New Delhi

FOREWORD

Laughter is a gift of nature. It energizes the being, electrifies the body, stirs up every fibre, and opens the windows to the brighter side of life.

This compilation of jokes aims at presenting to you the brighter and lighter side of life. Jokes in it have been collected for your enjoyment from every possible source around the world. These jokes include some naughty ones too: without them laughter would be anaemic and diluted. Interspersed among the jokes are some pithy sayings which might also make you smile.

Everybody is most welcome to reproduce any of these jokes and sayings: no need to acknowledge.

I am almost ninety years old. I have worked hard, laughed and enjoyed all along. Jokes have greatly helped. It is a great pleasure for me to reach this gift of laughter to you.

New Delhi

February 2001

H D SHOURIE

Three lawyers and three engineers were travelling by train to a conference. At the station, the three lawyers all bought tickets and watched as the three engineers bought one single ticket between them.

'How are you three people going to travel on a single ticket?' asked a lawyer.

'Wait and watch,' answered an engineer.

They all boarded the train. The lawyers took their respective seats, but all three engineers crammed into a toilet and closed the door behind them. Shortly after the train departed, the conductor came around, collecting tickets. He knocked on the toilet door and asked, 'Ticket, please.' The door opened just a crack and a single arm emerged with a ticket in hand. The conductor took it and moved on. The lawyers saw this and agreed it was a clever idea. So recognizing the engineers' superior intellect, after the conference, the lawyers decided to copy them on the return trip and save some money.

When they got to the station, they bought a single ticket for the return journey. To their astonishment, the engineers did not buy a ticket at all. 'How are you going to travel without even a single ticket?' asked one of the perplexed lawyers.

'Wait and watch,' answered an engineer.

When they boarded the train, the three engineers crammed into a toilet. The three lawyers crammed into another nearby. The train departed. Shortly afterwards one of the engineers left the toilet and walked to the other toilet where the lawyers were hiding.

He knocked on the door and said, 'Ticket, please.'

❖

Two friends were having lunch at a cafe. They noticed a man sitting alone at an adjoining table. When the waitress approached him, they overheard her ask, 'Are you waiting to be joined by a tall thin woman with long, blonde hair?'

He answered, 'In the larger scheme of life, yes. But today I'm meeting my wife.'

❖

A farmhand went to the doctor with a broken leg. . .

'Well, doc, twenty-five years ago. . .'

'Never mind the past. Tell me how you broke your leg this morning.'

'Like I was saying. . . twenty-five years ago, when I started working on the farm, that night, after I had gone to bed, the farmer's beautiful daughter came into my room. She asked me if there was anything I wanted. I said, "No, everything's fine." "Are you sure?" she asked. "I'm sure," I said. "Isn't there anything I can do for you?" she wanted to know. "I reckon not," I replied. . .'

'Excuse me,' said the doctor, 'What does this story have to do with your leg?'

The farmhand explained, 'Well, this morning when it dawned on me what she meant, I fell off the roof!'

❖

A woman who went to the police station to report her husband missing, described him as 'twenty-nine years old, 190 centimetres tall, fit and handsome.'

'I know your husband,' pointed out the desk sergeant. 'He is forty-eight, short and overweight.'

'Sure he is,' the woman answered. 'But who wants him back?'

❖

A person once went to the doctor for a follow-up examination. When asked if he had any problems since his last visit, he thought for a while, then he answered,

'Now that you mention it, I did have a flat tyre a couple of weeks ago.'

❖

As a child, a man had lost the sight in his right eye during a playground mishap. When he reached his forties, he needed to get glasses. At the optometrist's office, the doctor's young assistant pointed to an eye chart and told him, 'Cover your right eye and read the line there.'

'I am blind in my right eye,' he replied. 'It's a glass eye.'

'Okay,' the assistant responded. 'In that case, cover your left eye.'

❖

On Christmas Eve, a Christian mother who lives in Mumbai received a long-distance call from her daughter in Atlanta, USA. Barely had she started talking when her granddaughter Anjali, six, came on the line to list the gifts she wanted. The mother could hear her daughter repeatedly saying 'Anjali, that's enough.'

Finally Anjali snapped back, 'Mama, stop interrupting me. Don't you know this call costs a lot of money?'

❖

'If we are a country committed to free speech,' asks a critic, 'then why do we have phone bills?'

❖

Maid: What do you want, sir?
Visitor: I want to see your master.
Maid: What's your business, please?
Visitor: There is a bill. . .
Maid: Ah! He left yesterday for his village. . .
Visitor: Which I have to pay him. . .
Maid: And he returned this morning.

❖

After extensive tests, a person was told that his hearing ability was well above average. The technician was curious to know why anyone with perfect hearing would undergo these procedures.

'Well,' he replied sheepishly, 'my wife sent me because she claims I never hear a word she says.'

❖

The cleaning lady of the bank gave notice to the branch manager saying, 'You don't trust me.'

The branch manager replied, 'How can you say that? I even leave the keys of the safe lying around.'

Said the cleaning lady, 'That's true, but none of them fit.'

❖

Money is not everything. There's MasterCard and Visa.

An elderly man lay moaning in his bed in dying agony; he suddenly smelt the aroma of his favourite chocolate cookie, coming from the kitchen.

He gathered his remaining strength and lifted himself from the bed. Leaning against the wall, he slowly made his way out of the bedroom, and with even greater effort forced himself down the stairs gripping the railing with both hands.

With laboured breath, he leaned against the doorframe, gazing into the kitchen. Were it not for his dying agony, he would have thought himself already in heaven. There, spread out upon newspapers on the kitchen table, were literally hundreds of his favourite chocolate cookies!

Was it heaven? Or was this a final act of heroic love from his devoted wife, for ensuring that he left this world a happy man?

Mustering a great final effort, he threw himself towards the table, landing on his knees in a rumpled posture. The aged and withered hand shakingly made its way to a cookie at the edge of the table, when it was suddenly smacked with a spatula by his wife.

'Stay out of those,' she said. 'They're for the funeral.'

❖

Two men met in heaven. 'What did you die of?' asked the one.

'I died of extreme cold. And what about you?'

'I came home from work and heard my wife talking to a stranger. On entering the house I searched every nook and corner of the house but could not find anyone anywhere. I felt so guilty of my behaviour that my heart failed.'

At this, the other one said, 'Had you cared to open the fridge, neither of us would have died.'

❖

VIPs in the disturbed country on the hit list had been sent an elaborate set of don'ts to elude terrorists on their trail. Of these the most important was not to follow a regular routine but vary their timings and change their habitat as often as possible, e.g., don't go for your morning or evening walk at the same time to the same park, don't go to the same hotel or restaurant everyday etc. To these precautions, a wit who knew the habits of politicians there, added, 'Don't sleep in the same bed with the same person every night.'

❖

It was their second anniversary; The husband sent her flowers. He told the florist to write on the card: 'Happy Anniversary! Year Number 2. Love.' She was thrilled with the flowers, but not pleased about the card. It read, 'Happy Anniversary. You're number 2.'

❖

Men who treat women as helpless and charming playthings deserve women who treat men as delightful and generous bank accounts.

❖

A patient was lying nervously on the operating table waiting for the surgeon to arrive.

When he came, the patient blurted out: 'Doctor, I am very very nervous.'

'Don't be,' smiled the doctor.

'No doctor, I am very frightened, this is my first major operation,' the patient confessed.

'Mine too,' the doctor replied.

❖

Why do men get up in the middle of the night?

Any clue? No?

Well, a poll conducted in America

asked thousands of men the above question and got the following answer: two per cent men get up in the middle of the night to use the loo, three per cent to raid the refrigerator and ninety-five per cent get up to go home.

❖

A businessman in Florence in love with a nightclub entertainer employed a detective agency to check up on her. He received the following report: 'The young lady has an excellent reputation. Her past is without a blemish. She has many friends of good social standing. The only scandal associated with her is that she has often been seen lately with a businessman of questionable character.'

❖

A young couple was strolling hand in hand when they came upon a graveyard.

They decided to walk through it, and noticed that a woman was sitting beside a new grave and fanning it.

Said the husband to his wife: 'See, this is real love and devotion. Though her husband has died and gone, this woman is sitting by his grave and fanning him as though he were still alive.'

'Don't be too sure,' replied the wife. 'Let us go and ask her why she is doing it.'

So the couple walked up to the woman and said, 'Excuse us, no offence meant, but why are you doing this?'

The widow answered with moist eyes, 'My late husband was a very noble man. Before he died, he told me that I could go ahead and marry another man, but I should at least wait for the cement to dry on his grave. So I am sitting here and drying it.'

❖

Hard work spotlights the character of people: Some turn up their sleeves, some turn up their noses, and some don't turn up at all.

❖

One day during a war, a tall, strong and handsome Roman soldier broke into a house where he found two luscious maidens and their matronly nurse.

Chuckling with glee, he roared, 'Prepare thyselves for a conquest, my pretties.'

The lovely girls fell to their knees and pleaded with him, 'Do with us as thou wilt, O Roman, but spare our faithful old nurse.'

'Shut thy mouth,' snapped the old nurse. 'War is war.'

❖

A young man walked into a drugstore

that was being tendered by the owner's somewhat prudish wife.

'May I have six contraceptives, miss?' he asked.

'Don't "miss" me,' she replied.

'Okay,' the eager fellow said, 'make it seven.'

❖

Love thy neighbour. But don't get caught.

❖

The ardent honeymooning of her eighty-year-old groom was exhausting the young bride. During a momentary lull, while he was shaving, she sneaked out and staggered into the hotel coffee shop downstairs.

'I don't get it,' exclaimed her friend the waitress. 'Here you are, a teenage bride with an ancient husband, and you look a wreck, why?'

Yelled the young bride, 'The old goat double-crossed me. He told me he saved up for sixty years—and I thought he was talking about money!'

A tourist to India hired a clever guide to take him around Delhi and Agra. When taken to Red Fort at Delhi, he admired the architecture and asked how many years it took to build. The guide replied, 'Twenty years.' The tourist remarked, 'You Indians are a lazy lot. In my country, this could have been built in five years.' At the Taj he again admired its beauty and asked how many years it took to build. The guide reduced the period considerably and replied, 'Only ten years, sir.' The tourist retorted: 'Didn't I say you Indians are slow workers! In our country we can construct such buildings in two-and-a-half years.' Same story everywhere. He admired the architecture but reduced the period to one-fourth. The guide got irritated. When the taxi was nearing Qutab Minar, the tourist asked: 'What is that tower?' Came the reply, 'Sir, I will have to go and find out. When I was passing this way last evening, there was nothing there.'

❖

In the first year of marriage: The man speaks and the woman listens.

In the second year: The woman speaks and the man listens.

In the third year: they both speak and the neighbours listen.

❖

When his fourth son was born, the father invited his friend to join the celebration and choose a name for his newborn child.

'What names have you given to the three elder boys?' asked his friend.

'One is Rahmat Elahi (by God's kindness), the second Barkat Elahi (by God's grace) and the third Mahbubu Elahi (beloved of God),' replied the proud father.

The friend pondered over the names for a while and replied, 'I suggest you name your fourth son, Bas Kar Elahi (God, that is enough).'

❖

Overheard at the veterinarian's: 'I had my cat neutered. He's still out all night with the other cats, but now it's in the role of consultant.'

❖

In his autobiography, American comedian George Burns recalled: 'Of all the movies I've made, the only one that had me worried was the one that turned out to be my biggest hit. Oh, God! The minute I accepted the role, I started to panic. Should I be the one to play God? We're both about the same age, but we grew up in different neighbourhoods. What kind of voice should I use? I was very confused, so I looked up and hollered, "How do you play God?" There was no answer.

'The closer we got to the starting date, the more nervous I got. Then one night, I realized that no matter what, I couldn't be criticized. Nobody has ever seen Him, so who would know if I played Him right or wrong? That changed my whole attitude. Now I couldn't wait to get going. The week before shooting began, I rehearsed day and night—before dinner, after dinner, during dinner, while driving, while exercising. I got so into the role, that one night, when I said my prayers, I realized that I was talking to myself.'

❖

'**M**e sleep with Daddy last night,' the kid told her kindergarten teacher.

'I slept with Daddy last night,' the teacher corrected.

'Then you must have got into bed after I fell asleep,' the child answered.

❖

A couple hired a new chauffeur. The Memsahib asked him to take her out for shopping and was very shaken by the experience. Back home she pleaded with her husband, 'Please dear, you must sack this new chauffeur at once. He drives so rashly, he nearly killed me three times this morning.'

'Darling, don't be so hasty,' replied the husband, 'give him one more chance.'

❖

When an efficient secretary asked her boss for a raise in her salary, he rejected the case, and said: 'Your salary is already higher than the secretary's at the next desk. And she has five children, you know.'

'Excuse me,' she countered, 'I thought we got paid for what we produce here—not for what we produce at home in our own time.'

❖

Behind every successful man, there's a woman. Behind every unsuccessful man, there are two women.

❖

After twenty years, two college rivals bumped into each other. 'Do you remember how I used to be so fat and flabby?' asked the first. 'Well, I've been on an exercise programme for a few years, and now I run marathons.'

'That's great!' replied the other man.

'And,' the first man continued, 'do you

remember how I used to be a shy and poor student? Well, I took a course in public speaking, and now I make hundreds of thousands of dollars a year on the lecture circuit.'

'That's great!' came the reply.

'Oh! And how about you?' the first man enquired. 'Have you changed at all?'

'Yes, I have,' said the second man. 'Remember how brutally honest I used to be, and how, when someone said something uninteresting, I would reply, "I couldn't care less"? Well, now I just say, "That's great."'

❖

Overheard: 'A thief just ran off with my wallet,' yelled the champion runner.

'Couldn't you catch him?' asked the bystander.

'Sure, I even took the lead, but when I looked back, he was gone.'

❖

A small farm boy was milking his cow when all of a sudden a bull tore his chain and made straight for the cow. The boy was not at all afraid and continued with his milking while workers nearby watched in horror.

The bull came rushing in, then stopped equally suddenly but within a few inches of the boy, then turned round and walked away quietly. 'Weren't you afraid?' one of the workers asked the boy.

'Oh, not at all,' the boy replied coolly. 'I happened to know that this cow was his mother-in-law.'

❖

Boss: I can assure you that the value of the average employee will continue to increase.
Employee: That's because there will be fewer of us doing more work, right?
Boss: Right. Except for the 'us' part.

❖

A man came into the bar and ordered one whisky; when he had finished, the barman said, 'That's all right, no charge.' The man was surprised but delighted, so he ordered a sandwich and another whisky. When he offered to pay, the bartender said, 'That's all right, no charge.'

'I don't get it,' said the man astonished.

'You see,' explained the barman, 'my boss is upstairs doing to my girl what I'm doing to his business downstairs.'

❖

'It's a very difficult case to diagnose,' the doctor told the young brunette after finishing examination. 'As near as I can tell you're either going to have a baby or else you have a cold.'

'Must be a baby,' the girl said. 'I don't know anybody who could have given me a cold.'

❖

A patient was anxious after a prolonged bedside discussion by hospital doctors. When the head doctor came to see him he asked, 'There must be a lot of doubt about what is wrong with me.'

'Where did you get that idea?' the doctor replied.

'All the other doctors disagreed with you, didn't they?'

'To some extent, but don't worry,' said the doctor consolingly. 'In a similar case, I stood firm on my diagnosis, and the post-mortem proved me right!'

❖

Overheard: My accountant is worth every penny he charges because of the time he saves me. This year, for example, he probably saved me five to ten years in prison.

❖

A husband returning from a four-day hunting trip complained that he had lost his wedding ring.

'How did that happen?' asked his wife.

'It's your fault,' he replied. 'I've been telling you that all of my pockets have holes.'

❖

A Hindu, a Muslim and a Sikh were discussing the marvellous achievements of their brands of surgery.

The Hindu remarked: 'I know of a Vaidji, who joined a severed arm with the use of Ayurvedic glue. You can't even tell where the arm had been broken.'

Not to be outdone, the Muslim spoke: 'A hakeemsahib has evolved a new kind of adhesive ointment. He used it on a fellow who had his head cut off. You can't tell where the neck was severed.'

It was the Sardarji's turn now to extol the latest developments in Sikh surgery.

'We have gone much further,' said the Sardarji thumping his chest proudly. 'There was this Chacha of mine who was cut into two round his navel. Our Sikh surgeon immediately slaughtered a goat and joined its rear half to Chacha's upper half. So we have our Chacha as well as two litres of milk every day.'

❖

Animals are superior to human beings. There are thirty horses in a race and fifty thousand people go to see it; but put thirty people in a race and not one horse would go to see it.

❖

A man who had recently bought a female parrot with a salty vocabulary, got a call from his priest, telling him that he was planning to stop by the following week. Worried about the bird's language, he called a friend who had two well-behaved small birds. One recited the Lord's Prayer, while the other held a rosary in its claws and repeated Hail Marys.

'Would it be okay if I brought my bird over for a few days?' the man asked his buddy. 'Maybe my parrot will pick up some good habits from yours.' The friend agreed. So the man took his female parrot over, and put her in the cage next to that of the two devout males.

Suddenly, the first male parrot stopped praying and turned to the other. 'You can knock it off now,' he said. 'We've got what we were praying for.'

❖

Mr and Mrs Pawal once went to see a picture. In one of the scenes the hero of the film made passionate love to the heroine. Seeing this Mrs Pawal asked her husband, 'Darling, why don't you love me as much as he does in the picture?'

'Oh, keep shut. He is a professional and gets paid for it.'

❖

The taxi came to a sudden stop in the middle of the street.

'What's the matter?' called the young man from the rear seat.

'I thought I heard the young lady say "stop",' answered the driver.

'Oh, drive on, she wasn't talking to you.'

❖

A patient complains to a famous psychologist: 'Professor, I've been having terrible obsessions for years, and no one has ever been able to help me.'

'Well now, who treated you before?'

'Dr Lal Rathor.'

'I see. He's an idiot. I'm curious to know what he advised you to do.'

'That I should come and see you.'

❖

Overheard: I can say one good thing about airline food: at least they're considerate enough to give you only small portions.

❖

Why do you always insist on talking about the weather to your barber?'

'You wouldn't have me talk about anything as exciting as politics, to a man who is handling a razor, would you?'

❖

A Calcutta flat dweller called up a bird-shop the other day and said, 'Please send me fifty thousand cockroaches.'

'What for?'

'I'm moving today, and my lease says

I must have the flat in exactly the same condition in which I found it.'

❖

'**F**or the last time,' a husband shouted towards the bedroom, 'are you ready to go?'

'For heaven's sake, be quiet,' retorted his wife. 'I've been telling you for the last hour that I'll be ready in a minute.'

❖

Two terrorists were driving to the location where they intended to plant a time bomb, which one of them had in his lap.

'Drive a little faster, the bomb may go off any minute,' said the man carrying the explosive.

'Don't worry,' assured the driver, 'we have got a spare one in the boot.'

❖

When he got home, a man found his pregnant wife in labour, so he phoned the hospital. 'My wife is having contractions and they are two minutes apart, what should I do?' he asked frantically.

'Is this her first child?' asked the doctor.

'No!' the man shouted. 'This is her husband.'

❖

Boy to mother: 'I've decided to stop studying.'

'How come?' asked the mother.

'I heard the news that someone was shot dead downtown, because he knew too much.'

❖

In the taxi going to his hotel, an inebriated tourist took off his jacket and tie, and began to unbutton his shirt. The driver yelled back, 'Please stop undressing, sir, we're not at your hotel yet.'

'We're not?' mused the man. 'You might have told me sooner. I've already put my shoes outside the door.'

❖

The glory of great men should always be measured by the means through which they have acquired it.

❖

Husband: After I get up in the morning and shave, I feel ten years younger.

Wife: Why don't you shave before you go to bed?

❖

'There now,' cried little Christine the other day, rummaging through a drawer in the bureau, 'Grandma has gone to heaven without her spectacles.'

❖

Three snails decided one day to have coffee at a hotel. Just as they entered the cafe, it started raining. The elder of the three snails said to the smallest, 'Go home and bring an umbrella.'

The little one said, 'I will go, provided you don't drink my cup of coffee.'

'We won't,' promised the other two.

Two years later the big snail said to the middle one: 'Well, I guess he isn't coming back, so we might as well drink his coffee.' Just then a voice called from outside the door: 'If you do, I won't go.'

❖

A man who wanted to sell his car phoned a newspaper and asked how much it cost to put an ad in the paper.

'Two thousand rupees for 2.5 centimetres,' the man on the phone answered.

'I can't afford it then,' said the caller. 'My car is four and a half metres long.'

For their first anniversary, a man bought his young wife a cell phone. She was thrilled and listened eagerly as he explained all its features. The next day she was out shopping when the phone rang.

'Hey, darling,' her husband said. 'How do you like your new phone?'

'Oh, I just love it!' she gushed. 'It's so cute and small—and your voice sounds so clear. But there's just one thing I don't understand.'

'What's that?'

'How did you know I was at the sari shop?'

❖

The new bride was anything but tidy, and the husband had got used to finding the house in a mess. One evening, however, he returned home to find the place sparkling clean; The wife had finally got down to it. 'Darling,' he cried in dismay, 'what did you do with the dust that was on the table? I had a phone number scribbled on it.'

❖

A small post office in a desert town returned a letter to the sender with the remark:

'Addressee dead over a year. Left no forwarding address.'

❖

One morning a government clerk sat at the table after breakfast, engrossed in his newspaper for over an hour. Finally he asked for another cup of coffee.

'Coffee!' echoed his wife. 'But look at the time. Aren't you going to the office today?'

'Office?' exclaimed the startled man. 'Heaven! I thought I was at the office.'

❖

A miserly businessman who was away from his house, sent his wife a cheque for a million kisses. The wife, sent back the reply which read: 'Dear Murli: Thanks for the birthday cheque. The milkman cashed it this morning.'

❖

'Darling, how many times a day do you shave?'

'Twenty or thirty.'

'Are you crazy?'

'No. I'm a barber.'

❖

An English couple in a French cafe ordered chicken and were given a leg each. The English woman didn't want the leg piece and said she much preferred breast-meat.

The Englishman handed back the leg of chicken to the waitress, who didn't understand what he wanted, until he pointed at her bosom.

So she brought him a glass of milk.

❖

'Your marriage won't work,' warned a friend of the eighty-year-old man who had just wed a teenager. 'The age difference will soon cause a separation!'

'What is your advice?' asked the ancient groom.

'When you return from your honeymoon, advertise for a boarder. It'll help!'

The suggestion sounded good, and the old benedict followed it. A month later, the friend returned and inquired about the bride.

'She's fine and expecting!' the old buck answered.

'And how is that boarder of yours?' asked his pal.

'Wonderful, and by heck, she's expecting too!'

A Protestant minister, a Catholic priest, and a rabbi are talking about what they do with the money in the collection plate. The minister says: 'I draw a circle on the ground, close my eyes and throw the contents of the tray in the air; whatever falls in the circle, I give to God, the rest I keep.'

The priest says: 'I too draw a circle on the ground and throw the contents in the air. Any coin that stands on end, I give to God.'

The rabbi says: 'You sure make things complicated. I just put the collection on the table and tell God to take whatever he wants. The rest I keep.'

❖

A woman getting off a bus was seen deliberately to place a parcel on the seat. A fellow passenger, alighting at the time, asked her what she was doing.

'I do it every day,' was the reply. 'It's

my husband's lunch. He works in the Lost
Property Office.'

❖

'Now tell me about the dream you had,'
the psychiatrist said to the young lady on
the couch.

'Well I dreamt that I was walking
down the street with nothing on but a hat.'

'And you were embarrassed?'
suggested the doctor.

'Indeed I was!' agreed the lady. 'It was
last year's hat.'

❖

One of the guests turned to the man by
his side, and started criticizing the woman
at the piano.

'What a hoarse voice. Do you know
who she is?'

'Yes,' the neighbour replied. 'She is
my wife.'

Feeling embarrassed, the guest remarked, 'Oh! I beg your pardon. Of course, it is not her voice that's to blame. It's the song she has to sing. I wonder who wrote that terrible song.'

'I did,' came the answer.

❖

The lady of the house suspected that one of her two sons was paying attention to the maid. Anxious to find out which one, she said to the girl, 'Gertie, suppose you could have a date with one of my sons, which would you prefer?'

'Well,' replied Gertie, 'it's hard to say, Ma'am, for I've had some grand times with both of them. But for a real rollicking spree, give me the master.'

❖

A fine place to have a boil is on the bottom of the foot; nobody can step on it but yourself.

A man complained to his colleague, I have a severe headache and want some medicine to cure it.'

The colleague reassuringly remarked, 'You don't need any medicine. I had a headache yesterday, and when I went home, my loving wife just kissed me and comforted me, and the pain was soon off. Why don't you try the same cure?'

'Yes. I think I will. Is your wife at home now?'

❖

An absent-minded professor took a room at a boarding house. A few days later, he knocked on his landlady's door in a state of agitation. 'I cannot stay here unless you send a full-length mirror to my room immediately.'

'But why? That half-length mirror is brand new,' replied the landlady.

'It simply won't do,' retorted the professor. 'I keep going out without my pants on.'

The gay old bachelor was being examined by a doctor after fainting several times in a cocktail lounge.

After giving the middle-aged man a thorough medical examination, the doctor warned him that he would have to keep regular habits. 'But I do,' the patient protested.

'Is that so?' said the doctor with some scepticism. 'Then how did I happen to see you with the voluptuous redhead at three this morning?'

'That's one of my regular habits!'

❖

A guy is at the pearly gates, waiting to be admitted, while St.Peter is leafing through the big book to see if he is worthy of entering. St.Peter goes through the book several times, furrows his eyes, and says, 'I can't see anything good that you did in your life, but I can't see anything bad either. Tell you what, if you can tell me one really good thing you did in your life, you are in.'

The guy thinks for a moment and says: 'Yeah, there was this one time when I was driving down the highway and I saw a gang of rapists assaulting a poor girl. I slowed down my car to see what was going on, and sure enough, there they were, about seven of them, torturing this chick. Infuriated, I got out of my car, grabbed an iron rod out of the trunk, and walked straight up to the leader of the gang, a huge guy in a leather jacket. As I walked up to him, the gang of rapists formed a circle around me.

'So, I ripped the chain off the leader's face and smashed the iron rod on his head. Then I turned around and yelled to the rest of them, "You're all a bunch of sick, deranged animals. Go home before I teach you all a lesson."'

St.Peter, impressed, says: 'Really! When did this happen?'

'Oh, about two minutes ago before my

reaching these gates.'

❖

Customer: What do you have for greying hair?
Druggist: Nothing but the highest respect sir.

❖

Two fellows met at a restaurant. One of them was accompanied by his wife.

Said one to the other: 'Let me present my wife to you.'

'No thanks,' replied the other: 'I've got my own.'

❖

A young female job applicant was filling out an employment form in one of New York's larger public relations agencies. She had no trouble with the application until she came across a heading entitled: 'Sex.' She hesitated. Finally, she answered: 'Twice a week.'

❖

If you tell a man anything, it goes in one ear and out the other. And if you tell a woman anything, it goes in both ears and out of her mouth.

❖

A woman of thirty-five and a man in his forties had been going steady for fifteen years. One night she lifted her head from her pillow and said, 'Dear, let's get married.'

He lifted his head from his pillow and said, 'That's a good idea, honey, but who would want us?'

❖

The husband and wife were in the midst of a violent quarrel, and hubby was losing his temper. 'Be careful,' he said to his wife. 'You'll bring out the beast in me.'

'So what!' the wife replied. 'Who's afraid of a mouse?'

❖

In a swank club for men, one night, a dignified member walked in and was shocked when he saw women there for the first time.

'What happened?' he asked the club owner.

'We've decided to let members bring their wives in for dinner and dancing once a month,' was the reply.

'But that's not fair,' complained the member. 'I'm not married. Could I bring my girlfriend?'

The owner thought for a minute and replied slowly: 'I think it might be alright provided she's the wife of a member!'

'**I** want a divorce from my husband,' the lady stated bluntly.

'On what grounds?' her attorney inquired.

'I think he's been unfaithful to me,' she replied.

'And what makes you think he's been unfaithful?' asked the lawyer.

'Well, I don't think he's the father of my child.'

❖

The Dean of the women's college was lecturing to a class on the subject of sex morality.

'In moments of temptation, ask yourself just one question: Is an hour of pleasure worth a lifetime of shame?'

One of the girls raised her hand and naively asked, 'How do you make it last an hour?'

❖

If you can't say something nice become a reporter.

❖

Martin married a beautiful girl many years his junior. After a while he began to be torn by doubts as to her faithfulness, so he hired a private detective to watch her while he left on a business trip. On his return he called the detective.

'Out with it, out with it!' shouted Martin. 'I can take it. It's the element of doubt that's driving me crazy.'

'It looks bad,' said the detective. 'As soon as you left the house a handsome fellow called for your wife. I followed them to a nightclub. They had four or five drinks and then danced very close together. Then they went back to their table and held hands. Finally they took a cab back to your house. The lights were on, and I saw them walk into the bedroom and embrace. Then the lights went out and I couldn't see any more.'

'What did I tell you?' shouted Martin. 'That damned element of doubt!'

❖

Mr and Mrs Franke were seated at a night club table when a voluptuous redhead undulated past and nodded coldly at the man.

'Hello, Lola,' the husband answered.

'I suppose,' snapped his wife, 'you're going to tell me that Lola is an old school teacher of yours?'

'Don't be absurd,' said her husband. 'I wouldn't think of giving you such a ridiculous explanation. It might be good enough for Lola, though.'

❖

Jack: What's up Tim? You look troubled.
Tim: Yeah! I am going to be a father.
Jack: Congratulations. But what is so terrible about that, Tim?

Tim: Nothing—except my wife doesn't know it yet.

❖

One rainy night, a priest walked into a hotel and asked for a room. About an hour later, there was a knock on his door.

'Quick! Quick!' screamed the hotel manager, 'There's a terrible flood! Get yourself out in the rescue boat before you drown.'

But the priest remained calm. 'The Lord is my saviour. He will save me.'

Not long after this, the water had risen to the second floor. A second boat sailed past the priest's window, and the captain looked in. 'Good God, man! Jump in here before you die!' the captain screamed.

'The Lord is my saviour. He will save me,' answered the priest unperturbed. The waters rose higher and higher, until the priest was forced out of the house and onto the roof of the hotel. A helicopter saw his plight and dangled a rope ladder down to him. 'Hurry up, grab the ladder,' shouted the pilot.

'The Lord is my saviour. He will save me,' replied the priest again.

A gigantic lightning bolt struck the priest, and the next thing he knew, he was at heaven's gates, seated before God.

'My Lord, why did you forsake me!' he wailed.

'Forsake you! I sent you two boats and a helicopter, didn't I?'

❖

A man was sitting in a bar with tears streaming down his face. A friend walked in, and asked why he was so unhappy.

The weeping one said, 'The doctor has just told me I'll have to take these tablets for the rest of my life.'

Cheerfully, his friend pointed out that many people have to take tablets every day of their life.

'Sure,' came the reply, 'but he only gave me ten.'

❖

Ethel was shapely but shy, and visited a doctor for the first time. He ushered her into his private office, and said, 'And now, my dear, please get completely undressed.'

Ethel blushed and replied, 'Okay, doctor, but you first!'

❖

Benson and Ruth were on their honeymoon, riding in the day coach. They were passing through an exceptionally long tunnel and it was dark in the coach for quite some time. When they emerged into the daylight, Ben said, 'Ruthie, if I had known it would be dark so long, I'd have done it.'

Ruth cried, 'Benson! If you didn't, who did?'

How come wrong telephone numbers are never busy?

❖

A man leaves a bar, gets into his car and he's stopped by a police officer.

Officer: Sir, we're testing drivers for drunken driving. Would you please blow into this machine?

Man: I'm sorry, I can't do that. I have asthma. If I blow on that machine I will get out of air.

Officer: Please come along to the office and we can give you a blood test.

Man: I can't do that. I have anaemia and if you stick a needle in me I will bleed to death.

Officer: Then you'll have to get out and walk five yards along this white line.

Man: Can't do that either.

Officer: Why not?

Man: Because I'm dead drunk.

❖

Accept old age; it's a phase and a fact of life. There is a tale which says that, to begin with, God allotted to the man, the donkey, the dog, and the owl, thirty years each. While the others were content, man was not. Hence, God took about half the years from each of the others and gave them to man. Hence, for the first thirty years of his life, man lives a human life, but then, in succession, come the burdened years of the donkey, the snarling ones of the dog and the dozing ones of the owl.

Father : I'm worried about you always being at the bottom of your class.

Son: Don't worry, dad. They teach the same thing at both ends.

❖

A man from Chicago won a hundred thousand dollars in a weekend's gambling in Las Vegas, flew home, arriving at 3 a.m., made a deep hole in his backyard and buried the money there. Next morning, he went out and found the hole empty, and the money missing. Footsteps led from the hole to the house next door, where a deaf-mute lived.

Enraged, the man rushed to the house of a professor, who was qualified in the sign language of the deaf-mute and knew the man next door. He dragged the professor to the neighbour's house, held a gun against the head of the deaf-mute, then said to the professor: 'You tell this guy that if he does not return my hundred thousand dollars, I am shooting him.'

The professor conveyed the message to his friend, and the friend replied in sign language: 'Tell him not to shoot me. I have hidden the money under the cherry tree.' The professor turned to the man with the gun and said, 'He's not going to tell you. He says he'd rather die.'

❖

A man was driving home late one afternoon and he was driving above the speed limit. A police car suddenly emerged in the rear view mirror, sirens blaring. The man thought he would outpace it, so he pushed the accelerator to the floor and raced on. The two cars raced for some time, the speed rising to sixty, seventy, eighty, ninety, then the man said, what the heck, and pulled over, ready to receive a speeding ticket.

The police officer got out, leaned over the man and said: 'Listen, Mister, I have had a really lousy day, and I just want to go home. Give me a good excuse and I'll let you go.'

The man thought for a moment and said: 'Three weeks ago my wife ran off with a police officer. When I saw your car in my mirror, I thought you were the officer and you were trying to give her back to me.'

The officer let him go.

❖

A man is sitting quietly and reading his paper, when his wife sneaks up behind him and whacks him on the back of his head with a big frying pan.

Man: What was that for?

Wife: What was that piece of paper in your pant pocket with the name Marylou written on it?

Man: Oh honey, remember two weeks ago when I went horseracing? Marylou was the name of one of the horses I betted on.

Three days later, he is once again sitting reading the paper, when his wife repeats the swatting act with the frying pan.

Man: What was that for this time?

Wife: Your horse called last night.

❖

A guy goes to visit his grandmother and brings his friend along. While he is talking to his grandmother, the friend starts eating the peanuts on the table, and finishes them off. As they are leaving, the friend apologizes for finishing off the peanuts.

'That's all right,' says the grandmother, 'since I lost my dentures, I only suck the chocolate off them.'

❖

Two hunters got a pilot to fly them into the far north for elk hunting. They were quite successful and bagged six big bucks.

The pilot came back, as arranged, to pick them up. They started loading their gear into the plane, including the six elks. But the pilot objected and said, 'The plane can take only four of your elks, you'll have to leave two behind.' They argued with him, the year before they had shot six and the pilot allowed them to put all six aboard, and the plane was just the same model and capacity as this. Reluctantly the pilot permitted them to put all six aboard. But when the plane attempted to clear the hills, it could not make it and it crashed in the wilderness. Climbing out of the wreckage, one hunter said to the other, 'Do you know where we are?'

'I think so,' replied the other hunter. 'I think this is about the same place where the plane crashed last year.'

❖

Young boy to his friend: 'First they tell you, you're guaranteed privacy under the Constitution, and then they send your report card to your parents.'

❖

A busy working Mum, a woman tried to pack in as many errands into the lunch break as possible. One day at noon time, she raced to get a chest X-ray done at the hospital, then went to the cleaners, and finally, the supermarket. When she returned to the office, she noticed strange looks from the co-workers. Eventually the boss enquired what she did during lunch, and, after explaining the hectic hour, she asked, 'Why do you want to know?'

'Well,' the boss said, 'your blouse is inside out.'

❖

At the end of a job interview, the human resources director asked the new MBA graduate what salary he would expect if he were hired. The candidate responded confidently, 'In the neighbourhood of one lakh rupees per month, depending on the benefits package.'

The human resources director replied, 'What would you say to a benefits package of five paid weeks of vacation, fourteen paid holidays, full medical and dental, a retirement fund with a fifty percent company match, and a company car—say a BMW.'

The new MBA sat up, mouth agape,

and said, 'Are you kidding?'

'Of course,' the director replied. 'But you started it!'

❖

The boss called an employee into his office and said, 'Ram, you have been with the company for a year. You started in the mail room. One week later, you were promoted to a sales position, and one month after that, you were promoted to district manager of the sales department. Just four short months later, you were promoted to vice president. Now it's time for me to retire, and I want to make you the new president and CEO of the corporation. What do you say to that?'

'Thanks,' said the employee.

'Thanks?' the boss replied. 'Is that all you can say?'

'I guess not,' the employee said. 'Thanks Dad.'

❖

God decided it was time to end the world, so he called together those whom he considered the three most influential people in the world—Bill Clinton, Fidel Castro and Bill Gates.

'The world will end,' God told them. 'You must go and tell the people.'

President Clinton made a live statement on CNN. 'I have good news and bad news,' he said. 'The good news is that we have been right, there is a God. The bad news is that he is ending the world.'

Castro sent out a worldwide message to all Communists. 'I have bad news and worse news,' he said. 'The bad news is that we have been wrong all along—there is a God. The worse news is that he is ending the world.'

Bill Gates got on his computer and sent out a worldwide e-mail on the Internet. 'I have good news and better news,' he wrote. 'The good news is that God thinks I'm one of the three most influential people in the world. The better news is that we don't have to upgrade anymore.'

❖

A panda walked into a restaurant and ordered a sandwich and a drink. When he finished, he pulled out a pistol and shot up the place, scaring customers and breaking dishes, glasses and liquor bottles before turning to leave.

Shocked, the manager said, 'Hey, what are you doing?'

The Panda glanced back over his shoulder and said, 'I'm a panda—look it up,' before disappearing through the door. The bartender pulled out a dictionary and thumbed through it until he found an entry for Panda. The definition read, 'A tree-dwelling animal of Asian origin characterized by distinct black-and-white markings. Eats shoots and leaves.'

❖

Late one night, a mugger wearing a ski mask jumped into the path of a well-dressed man and stuck a gun in his ribs. 'Give me your money,' he demanded.

Indignant, the affluent man replied, 'You can't do this—I'm a politician!'

'In that case,' replied the robber, 'give me my money!'

❖

An American visiting England walked into a hotel lobby and pushed a button for elevator service. 'The lift will be down presently,' said a nearby clerk.

'The lift?' said the American. 'Oh, you mean the elevator.'

'No, I mean the lift,' replied the Englishman, annoyed by the American arrogance.

'I think I should know what it is called,' said the American. 'Elevators were invented in the States.'

'Perhaps,' retorted the Englishman.

'But the language was invented by us.'
Doctor: Did you take my advice about your insomnia and count before going to sleep?

Patient: Yes, Doctor, I got as far as 24,534 and then it was time to get up.

❖

If you aim at nothing you'll hit it every time.

❖

A pop guitarist living in a small apartment was rehearsing one night when he heard his new next door neighbour pounding on the wall. He turned down the amplifier, but still the pounding continued. Hoping to establish a friendly relationship, he stopped playing, walked over to her door and rang the bell so that he could apologize.

'Oh, I'm so very sorry,' she said, looking frazzled as she opened her door and saw him standing there. 'I only have one more picture to hang.'

❖

While browsing in a bookstore, a man overheard a customer ask a saleswoman where the computer-book section was located. The employee directed her to the back corner of the store and asked, 'Is there something specific you are looking for?'

'Yes,' the woman replied. 'My husband.'

❖

A busload of politicians was driving down a country road all going to the local constituency to battle out the coming elections. Suddenly, the bus ran off the road and crashed into a tree in an old farmer's field. Seeing what had happened, the old farmer rushed to the spot. He then proceeded to dig a hole and bury the politicians.

The next day the local police came to the scene to investigate. They asked the old farmer: 'You buried all of them. . .but were they all dead?'

The old farmer replied: 'Well, some of them said they weren't, but you know how them politicians lie!'

❖

One Sunday morning the daughter burst into the house and said, 'Dad! Mom! I have some great news for you: I am getting married to the greatest hunk in Washington. He lives in Georgetown and his name is Matt.'

After dinner, the father took the daughter aside. 'Honey, I have to talk with you. Your Mother and I have been married a long time. She's a wonderful wife, but I have fooled around with some women. Matt is actually your half-brother, and I'm afraid you can't marry him.'

The daughter was heartbroken, but after eight months, she eventually started dating again. A year later, she came home and very proudly announced: 'Robert asked me to marry him; we're getting married in June.'

Again her father insisted on another private conversation and broke the sad news to her. 'Robert is your half-brother too, honey. I'm awfully sorry about this.'

The daughter was furious; she finally decided to go to her mother and tell her. 'Dad has done so much harm. I guess I'm never going to get married,' she complained. 'Every time I fall in love, Dad tells me the guy is my half-brother.' Mother just shook her head. 'Don't pay any attention to what he says, dear. He's not really your father.'

❖

'I'm very sorry to learn that your wife

ran away with your driver,' said the friend
to the old man.

'Oh, don't worry, I can drive myself,
anyway.'

❖

Two ladies were discussing what they
should wear to the country club dance.

'We're supposed to wear something to
match our husband's hair. So I'm going to
wear black,' said Mrs Johnson.

'Goodness', gasped her companion. 'I
don't think I'll go.' Her husband was bald.

❖

'Daddy, what does "alternative" mean?'
a little boy asks his father.

The older man sits his son down and
says: 'Imagine you're a young man and
want to start a business. One day you
decide to buy a hen. The hen starts to lay
eggs. In time the chicks hatch, and you

now have a lot of chickens. You're rich, you own a chicken farm, cars, horses. . .'

'Daddy,' interrupts the son impatiently, 'but I wanted to know what "alternative" meant.'

'Yes son. That's what I'm trying to explain. So you're a rich man now, but one day a huge flood takes your farm away. You lose everything and your chickens drown because the stupid birds can't swim.'

'What about "alternative", Daddy?'

'The alternative, my son, is ducks.'

❖

A judge looked severely at the defendant and asked, 'How many times have you been imprisoned?'

'Nine, your Honour.'

'Nine? In this case, I will give you the maximum sentence.'

'Maximum sentence?' replied the defendant. 'Don't give your regular clients a discount?'

❖

A surgeon, an architect and a politician were discussing which of their professions was the oldest. 'Mine, certainly', said the surgeon, 'for it was inaugurated by God when he removed man's rib to make woman.'

'But before making man and woman,' the architect said, 'he had to be an architect to give form to the creation, producing it from chaos.'

'Exactly,' said the politician, 'and who made the chaos?'

❖

One man to another: 'I want to marry a smart woman, a good woman; a woman who'll make me happy.'

'Make up your mind.'

❖

The bride and groom drifted out to sea, caught by an undertow that carried their boat beyond sight of land. The groom became frantic and began to pray.

'Oh Lord, if you will wash us back to shore,' he prayed, 'I'll quit smoking, gambling, drinking. . .'

'Don't go too far, dear,' shouted his bride. 'I think I see a sail.'

❖

The prudish old maid found herself seated next to a sophisticated playboy at a formal affair. After a little, rather icy conversation, the lady attempted to dismiss the fellow, 'Its quite obvious, sir, that we do not agree on a single, solitary thing.'

The playboy smiled. 'Oh, I don't think that's quite true, madam,' he said. 'If you were to enter a bedroom in which there were two beds, and if madam, there was a woman in one and a man in the other, in which bed would you sleep?'

'Well', the lady huffed indignantly. 'With the woman, of course.'

'You see, we agree,' the playboy said laughing. 'So would I.'

❖

The ship's captain returned from a two-year voyage to find his wife nursing a month-old baby. 'Who did this?' he demanded. 'Was it my friend Mike Fitzpatrick?'

'No,' his wife said softly.

'Well then, was it my friend Bob Bigelow?'

His wife shook her head.

'Bill Connery?' he demanded. 'Could it have been my friend Bill Connery?'

'Your friends, your friends,' his wife said impatiently, 'all the time, your friends. Don't you think I have any friends of my own?'

❖

The two office workers were complaining about the short lunch hours.

'The boss takes an hour-and-a-half every day and expects us to get by in thirty minutes,' said Tom.

'If I had an extra fifteen, I could go home for lunch,' agreed Bill.

'The boss is never around at noon. Why don't we just take the extra fifteen minutes,' Tom suggested.

Bill agreed and that very day he went home for lunch. Naturally his wife wasn't expecting him and when he didn't find her in the front part of the house, Bill looked in the bedroom. When he opened the door, he discovered his wife in bed with his boss. Bill backed out of the room quietly, slipped out of the house without being noticed and hurried back to the office.

The following morning Tom asked him if he was going to take the extra fifteen minutes again that day.

'Hell, no,' said Bill. 'I almost got caught yesterday.'

A father was shopping in a department store with his small daughter, when the little girl suddenly pulled on his coat sleeve and said, 'Daddy, I gotta go.'

'In a few minutes, dear,' the father replied.

'I gotta go now,' the little girl insisted in a very loud voice.

To avoid a scene, a sales lady stepped forward and said, 'That's all right, sir, I'll take her.'

The saleslady and the little girl hurried off hand in hand. When they returned, the father asked his daughter, 'Did you thank the nice lady for being so kind?'

'Why should I thank her,' retorted the little girl as loud as before. 'She had to go, too.'

❖

A lovely young lady entered a doctor's office in lunch hour and addressed a handsome young man in a white coat. 'I've had a pain in my shoulder for a week. Can you help me?'

'Lie down on this table,' he said, 'and I'll massage it for you.' After several minutes, the beauteous patient exclaimed, 'Doctor, that isn't my shoulder.'

The young man smiled and replied: 'No, and I'm not a doctor either.'

❖

Men who are getting on in years should console themselves with the thought that when they get too old to set bad examples, they can always start giving advice.

❖

Some months ago, a rape case was being tried in a Hollywood court. The victim, a movie starlet, was on the stand. 'Now then, young lady,' the prosecutor began, 'Please tell the court, in your own words, just what happened. First of all, can you identify the man?'

'That's the one,' said the girl, pointing.

'And can you tell the court when this occurred?'

'Yes, sir,' she replied thoughtfully. 'As I remember, it was last June, July, August and September.'

❖

A much-travelled playboy observes that the various stages of a woman's life resembles the continents of the world. From thirteen to eighteen, for example, she's like Africa—virgin territory, unexplored. From eighteen to thirty, she's like Asia—hot and exotic. From thirty to forty-five, she's like America—fully explored and free with her resources. From forty-five to fifty-five, she's like Europe—exhausted, but not without points of interest. After fifty-five, concludes the playboy, she's like Australia—everybody knows it's down there, but nobody cares much.

❖

Before he went off to the wars, King Arthur locked his lovely wife, Guinevere, into her chastity belt. Then he summoned his loyal friend and subject, Sir Lancelot.

'Lancelot, noble knight,' said Arthur, 'within this sturdy belt is imprisoned the virtue of my wife. The key to this chaste treasure I will entrust to only one man in the world. To you.'

Humbled before this great honour, Lancelot knelt, received his king's blessing, and took charge of the key. Arthur mounted his steed and rode off. Not half-a-mile from his castle, he heard hoofbeats behind him and turned to see Sir Lancelot riding hard to catch up with him. 'What is amiss, my friend?' asked the king.

'My lord,' gasped Lancelot, 'you have given me the wrong key!'

❖

A very plain nurse was telling a voluptuous co-worker about the sailor who was a patient in ward ten. 'He's tattooed,' she confided (and her voice dropped low), 'in a very intimate place!'

'You mean. . .' gasped the beautiful nurse.

'Yes! Isn't that odd? There's actually a word tattooed there. The word "swan".'

'This I've got to see', exclaimed the voluptuous one, and she hurried off to ward ten. Half-an-hour later, she returned. 'You were right,' she said, 'he is tattooed there. But you were wrong about the word. It's "Saskatchewan".'

❖

It is said that a team of researchers on

the sexual habits of the city dwellers interviewed a cross section of city's business community. Among the questions posed to them, one was: What do you do immediately after you have had sex? The answers were most revealing. Ten per cent replied that they simply went to sleep. Another ten per cent replied that they washed themselves and took some nourishment—a glass of fruit juice, aerated water or a sandwich. The remaining eighty per cent, after much cajoling replied: 'Then we go home.'

❖

Did you follow my advice about kissing your girl when she least expects it?' asked the sophisticated college senior of his younger fraternity brother.

'Oh, hell,' said the fellow with the swollen eye. 'I thought you said where.'

❖

It's usually a girl's geography that determines her history.

❖

Mrs Fransworthy felt sad but sympathetic when she got the news that Juliette, her jewel of a French maid was, leaving to get married.

'Ah, well,' she said, seeing the glow of happiness on the girl's beautiful young face, 'I am overjoyed for you, Juliette. You will have it much easier now that you're getting married. . .'

'Yes, madam,' said the girl with a tingle of anticipation that made her trim figure tremble, 'and more frequently as well.'

❖

Flustered and flushed, Carol sat in the witness chair. The beautiful but empty-headed blonde had got herself named correspondent in a divorce case and was presently being questioned in court.

'So, Miss Carol,' the lawyer intoned, 'you admit that you went to a hotel with this man?'

'Yes, I do, but I couldn't help it.'

'Couldn't help it? Why not?'

'He deceived me.'

'And how did he do that?'

'Well,' Carol said earnestly, 'he told the clerk at the reception desk that I was his wife.'

❖

Mrs Brown pulled Mrs Green out of earshot of the porch, where Mrs Green's lovely young daughter, Carol, sat.

'It's really none of my business,' whispered Mrs Brown, 'but have you noticed what your daughter is doing?'

'Carol?' Mrs Green responded apprehensively. 'Why, no. What's she up to?'

Mrs Brown leaned closer. 'She's knitting tiny garments,' she hissed.

Mrs Green's troubled brow cleared. 'Well, thank goodness,' she said, smiling. 'I'm glad to see she's taken an interest in something besides running around with boys.'

❖

A woman with a past attracts men who hope history will repeat itself.

❖

The newly-weds were obviously suffering from exhaustion, and after a routine examination their doctor advised: 'It's not unusual for a young couple to overdo things during the first weeks of marriage. What you both need is more rest. For the next month, I want you to limit your sexual activity to those days of the week with an r in them—that is

Thursday, Friday and Saturday.'

Since the end of the week was approaching the newly-weds had no immediate difficulty following the doctor's orders. But on the first evening of scheduled rest, the young bride found herself unusually passionate. Hubby fell asleep quickly, but she tossed and turned interminably and finally nudged her spouse into partial wakefulness.

Expecting daylight, and confused because it was still dark, he asked, 'What day is it?'

'Mondray,' said his bride, cuddling against him.

❖

'What are you nagging me about?' complained the husband. 'I was in last night by a quarter of twelve.'

'You were not, you liar!' cried the irate wife. 'I heard you come in and the clock was striking three.'

'Well, stupid,' said hubby. 'Isn't three a quarter of twelve?'

❖

In Rio on a business trip, Al found himself hampered after working hours by the fact that he didn't know the language. When a plunging neckline surrounded by femininity of surpassing comeliness sat down at his restaurant table, he was at once delighted and dismayed.

'Can you speak English?' he ventured hopefully.

'Si,' she said with a bright white smile. 'Bot jus a leetle beet.'

'Just a little bit, eh?' Al repeated jokingly. 'How much?'

'Twenty-five dollars,' was the prompt reply.

❖

The six fraternity men came weaving out

of the off-campus gin mill and started to crowd themselves into the little Volkswagen for the rollicking ride back home. One of them, obviously the house president, took charge of the situation.

'Herbie,' he said, 'You drive. You're too drunk to sing.'

❖

Sometimes a girl can attract a man by her mind, but more often she can attract him by what she doesn't mind.

Jack had shown Lousie his etchings and just about everything else of interest in his apartment. As he poured the last of the martinis into their glasses, he realized that the moment of truth with Louise had arrived. He decided on the direct verbal attack.

'Tell me,' he said smoothly, fingering a lock of her hair, 'do you object to making love?'

She turned her lovely eyes up to his

and said, 'That's something I've never done.'

'Never made love?' cried Jack, appalled at the waste of magnificent raw material.

'No, silly,' she said in soft rebuke. 'Never objected.'

❖

'I don't know what's wrong with me, Doctor,' said the curvy call girl. 'I feel tired, dragged out, pooped, no pep, no get up and go. Is it vitamin deficiency, low blood count or what?'

The medico gave her a tip-to-toe examination and then his verdict: 'Young lady, there's really nothing wrong with you. You're run-down, that's all. You've been working too hard. I suggest you try staying out of bed for a few days.'

❖

Everyone in the smart night-club was amazed by the old gentleman, obviously pushing seventy, tossing off Manhattans and cavorting around the dance floor like a twenty-year-old. Finally, curiosity got the better of the cigarette girl.

'I beg your pardon, sir,' she said, 'but I'm amazed to see a gentleman of your age living it up like a youngster. Tell me, are all of your faculties unimpaired?'

The old fellow looked up at the girl sadly and shook his head. 'Not all, I'm afraid,' he said. 'Just last evening I went night-clubbing with a girlfriend. We drank and danced all night and finally rolled into her place about 2 a.m. We went to bed immediately and I was asleep almost as soon as my head hit the pillow. I woke around 3.30 and nudged my girl. "Why, George," she said in surprise, "we did that just fifteen minutes ago."'

'So you see,' the old boy said sadly, 'my memory is beginning to fail me.'

❖

The none-too-bright young fellow had been dating the same girl for more than a year and one evening, the girl's father confronted him and wanted to know whether the lad's intentions toward his daughter were honourable or dishonourable.

'Gee,' said the young man, swallowing hard, 'I didn't know I had a choice!'

❖

The naive miss was seated in her doctor's office.

'Our tests indicate that you are pregnant,' said the doctor, 'and there is every indication that you are going to have twins.'

'But how can that be, Doctor?' the girl protested. 'I've never been out on a double date in my life.'

❖

The sweet young daughter was telling her mother about the great time she had at the mountain resort. 'I met a man in the recreation hall and we played Ping-Pong all afternoon. What fun, mother!'

'Why, dear,' remarked the mother. 'I never knew you enjoyed Ping-Pong.'

'I do now,' the daughter said. 'I'd hit the ball the wrong way and we'd both go after it under the table. Then he'd hit the ball the wrong way and we'd both go after it under the table. We played all afternoon. It was wonderful.'

'But I don't understand,' said the mother, 'where does the fun come in?'

'Under the table, silly.'

❖

Some girls marry old men for money and spend the rest of their lives looking for a little change.

❖

The rural lady had been coming into the city hospital regularly to give birth to her annual child. When she was packing up to go home after her tenth trip, the nurse said, 'Well, Mrs Slocum, I suppose we'll be seeing you again next year, as usual?'

'No, ma'am,' drawled Mrs Slocum. 'My husband and I just found out what's been causing it.'

❖

The doctor had just finished giving the young man a thorough physical examination.

'The best thing for you to do,' the doctor said, 'is give up drinking and smoking, get to bed early and stay away from women.'

'Doctor, I don't deserve the best,' said the patient. 'What's next best?'

❖

The husband wired home that he had been able to wind up his business trip a day early and would be home on Thursday. When he walked into his apartment, however, he found his wife in bed with another man. Furious, he picked up his bag and stormed out; he met his mother-in-law in the street, told her what had happened and announced that he was filing a suit for divorce in the morning.

'Give my daughter a chance to explain before you take any action,' the older woman pleaded. Reluctantly, he agreed.

An hour later, his mother-in-law phoned the husband at his club.

'I knew my daughter would have an explanation,' she said, a note of triumph in her voice. 'She didn't receive your telegram!'

❖

One of the airlines recently introduced a special half-fare rate for wives accompanying their husbands on business trips. Anticipating some valuable testimonials, the publicity department of the airline sent out letters to all the wives of businessmen who used the special rates, asking how they enjoyed their trip.

Responses are still pouring in asking, 'What trip?'

❖

'**A**re you sure this is your house?' the cop asked the thoroughly sozzled gentleman.

'Shertainly,' said the drunk, 'and if you'll just open the door f'me, I'll prove it to you.'

'You shee that piano?' the drunk began. 'Thash mine, you shee that television set? Thash mine, too. Follow me.'

The police officer followed as he shakily negotiated the stairs to the second floor. The drunk pushed open the first door they came to.

'Thish ish my bedroom,' he announced. 'Shee that bed? Shee that woman lying in the bed? Thash my wife. And shee that guy lying next to her?'

'Yeah,' said the cop suspiciously.

'Thash me!'

❖

The dazzling movie star was applying for her passport.

'Unmarried?' asked the clerk.

'Occasionally,' answered she.

❖

As they ran for their respective trains, Lal called to his fellow commuter, Paul: 'How about a game of golf tomorrow?'

'Sorry,' Paul called back, 'but it's the kids' day off, and I've got to take care of the maid.'

❖

Some girls ask the boss for advances on next week's salary. Others ask for salary on next week's advances.

❖

Latest comment from the pundits regarding the population explosion. If the birth rate keeps increasing, there will soon be standing room only on the earth, at which time the birth rate should stop increasing pretty quickly.

❖

A soldier who had married just before going overseas returned to the United States, filled with the desire to see his young bride. At his request his commanding officer granted him a special twenty-four-hour pass.

He didn't come back until another twenty-five hours had elapsed. His CO barked at him: 'What do you mean by overstaying your leave?'

'Well, sir,' said the trembling GI, 'when I got home, my wife was taking a bath.'

'Taking a bath!' shouted his CO. 'Does that take two days?'

'Well, no, sir. But you see, it took almost two days for my uniform to dry.'

❖

The party was a swinging affair. In the dimmed lights of the apartment, Joe spied a female form alone in a corner. He crept up behind her, and before she was aware of his presence, clasped her in a passionate embrace and kissed her soundly.

'How dare you!' she shrieked indignantly, pulling away.

'Pardon me,' Joe bluffed smoothly, 'I thought you were my sister.'

'You jerk,' she said tartly, 'I *am* your sister.'

❖

Two shapely stenographers were standing on a crowded subway. One asked the other: 'That man behind me—is he good-looking?'

'Well, he's young,' was the answer.

The first girl nodded. 'That I know.'

❖

While vacationing last summer in the North Woods, a young fellow thought, it might be a good idea to write to his girl. He had brought no stationery with him, however, so he had to walk into town for some. Entering the one and only general store, he discovered that the clerk was a young, full-blown farm girl with languorous eyes. 'Do you keep stationery?' he asked.

'Well,' she giggled, 'I do until the last few seconds, and then I just go wild.'

❖

Mrs Culpepper was almost in tears. 'Oh, Marie,' she said to her maid, 'I believe my husband is having an affair with his secretary.'

'I don't believe it,' snapped Marie. 'You're just saying that to make me jealous.'

❖

Give a man enough rope and he'll claim he's tied up at the office.

❖

A not too good-looking woman had her photograph taken and wasn't very pleased with the results. She complained to the photographer that his pictures didn't do her justice.

'Lady, you don't want justice,' said the photographer. 'You want mercy.'

❖

The young man addressed his prospective father-in-law: 'Sir, I would like to marry your daughter.'

'I'm afraid, son,' the older man replied, 'that you couldn't support her in the manner to which she is accustomed.'

'Your daughter and I have talked it over, and she has consented to live on what I earn.'

'That's fine. But remember that after a while a little one may come along, and that will mean added expense.'

'Well, that's true, sir,' the youth agreed, 'but we've been lucky so far.'

❖

'Darling,' she whispered, 'will you still love me after we are married?'

He considered this for a moment and then replied, 'I think so. I've always been especially fond of married women.'

❖

The sophisticated lady was approached on the dance floor by a gentleman slightly her junior.

'I'm sorry,' she said in a superior tone, 'but I cannot dance with a child.'

'Oh, I'm sorry,' he said. 'I didn't know about your condition.'

❖

One of our favourite bartenders told us about a very proper Englishman who came into his place a couple of weeks ago. The fellow sat down at the bar, but didn't order. The bartender, an unusually friendly guy, asked him if he could fix him a drink, on the house.

The Englishman shook his head. 'Tried liquor once,' he said. 'Didn't like it.'

The bartender then offered the Englishman a cigarette.

'No, thank you,' he said. 'Tried tobacco once. Didn't like it.'

Still trying to be friendly, the

bartender asked the Englishman if he would like to join a couple of friends seated at the bar in a few hands of poker.

The Englishman shook his head. 'Tried gambling once. Didn't like it. I wouldn't be sitting in this place at all, but I promised my son I would meet him here.'

'I see,' said the bartender. 'Your only child, I assume.'

❖

An old man, walking down the street, saw a small boy sitting on the curb crying. He stopped and asked, 'Little boy, why are you crying?'

The little boy said, 'I'm crying because I can't do what the big boys do.' So the old man sat down beside him and cried, too.

❖

Three decrepit grey-haired gentlemen were seated together in the park

'I'm eighty-six,' said the first, 'and I wouldn't be here today if I hadn't scorned tobacco and alcohol in every form, avoided late hours and the sinful enticements of the opposite sex.'

'I owe my ninety-three years to a strict diet of blackstrap molasses, wheat-germ bread and mother's milk,' said the second old man.

'When I was eighteen,' the third man said, 'my father told me that if I wanted to enjoy life as much as he had, I should smoke black cigars, drink nothing but hard liquor and carouse with a different woman every night. And that's exactly what I've done.'

'Incredible,' said the first old man.

'Amazing,' said the second, for their friend was obviously the greyest, most elderly appearing of the three, 'Just how old are you?'

'Twenty-two,' was the answer.

❖

A rather inebriated fellow on a bus was tearing up a newspaper into tiny pieces and throwing them out the window.

'Excuse me,' said the woman sitting next to him. 'But, would you mind explaining why you're tearing up that paper and throwing the pieces out of the window?'

'It scares away the elephants,' said the drunk.

'I don't see any elephants around here,' said the woman, smiling.

'Effective, isn't it?' said the drunk.

❖

An optimist is a man who looks forward to marriage. A pessimist is a married optimist.

❖

'Is something the matter?' asked the bartender of the young, well-dressed customer, who sat staring sullenly into his drink.

'Two months ago my grandfather died and left me eighty-five thousand dollars,' said the man.

'That doesn't sound like anything to be upset about,' said the bartender polishing a glass. 'It should happen to me.'

'Yeah,' said the sour young man, 'but last month an uncle on my mother's side passed away. He left me a hundred and fifty thousand dollars.'

'So why are you sitting there looking so unhappy?' asked the bartender.

'This month so far not a cent.'

❖

'Before we get married,' said the young man to his fiancee, 'I want to confess some affairs I've had in the past.'

'But you told me all about those a couple of weeks ago,' replied the girl.

'Yes, darling,' he explained, 'but that

was a couple of weeks ago.'

❖

Have you heard about the man who never worried about his marriage, until he moved from New York to California and discovered that he still had the same milkman?

❖

George knew just what he wanted in a woman. 'The girl I marry,' he used to tell us, 'will be an economist in the kitchen, an aristocrat in the living room and a harlot in bed.'

Now he's married and his wife has all the required traits—but not in the same order. She's an aristocrat in the kitchen, a harlot in the living room and an economist in bed.

❖

On the first night of their honeymoon

the bride slipped into a flimsy bit of silk and crawled into bed, only to find that her husband had settled down on the couch. When she asked him why he was apparently not going to make love to her, he replied, 'Because it's Lent.'

'Why, that's the most ridiculous thing I've ever heard,' she exclaimed, almost in tears. 'To whom, and for how long?'

❖

A stern father was taking his little son Johnny for a walk in the park when suddenly a honeybee settled on a rock in front of them. Just for spite, the boy smashed it with a rock, whereupon the father said, 'That was cruel, and for being cruel you'll get no honey for a whole year.'

Later, Johnny deliberately stepped on a butterfly. 'And for that, young man,' said the father, 'you'll get no butter for a whole year.'

When they returned home, Johnny's mother was busy fixing dinner. Just as they entered the kitchen, she spied a cockroach and immediately crushed it underfoot. The little boy looked at his father impishly, and said: 'Shall I tell her, Dad, or will you?'

❖

A young politician eager to gather votes, accepted the invitation of a local women's club to speak on the subject of sex. However, fearing that his wife wouldn't understand, he told her that he planned to lecture on sailing.

A week after the speech, his wife ran into one of the ladies of the club who mentioned how entertaining his talk has been.

'I just can't understand it,' said the wife. 'He knows so little about it.'

'Come now, darling. Don't be coy. His talk showed intimate acquaintance with the subject,' said the matron.

'But he's only tried it twice,' protested

the wife. 'The first time, he lost his hat and the second time he became seasick.'

❖

'**A**nd what do you two think you are doing?' roared the husband, as he came upon his wife in bed with another man.

The wife smiled at her companion. 'See?' she said. 'I told you he was stupid!'

❖

Calling on an attractive co-ed, the theology professor asked, 'Who was the first man?'

'It's all the same to you, sir,' replied the embarrassed co-ed, 'I'd rather not tell.'

❖

A polite and rather timid young man, after buying for a lady friend a pair of gloves as a birthday present, scribbled the following note to be sent along with them:

'I hope you find these a welcome birthday gift, since I noticed on our last few dates that you weren't wearing any. They are reversible, so if you get them soiled you can wear them inside out and thus wear them longer without having to wash them. I'm only sorry I cannot be there at your party to watch your smiling face as you try them on.'

He left the note with the sales lady, who promptly sent it off with the wrong package: a pair of silk panties.

❖

'But, Robert,' his wife gasped, 'why did you park here when there are so many nicer spots further down the road?'

He stopped what he was doing just long enough to mutter, 'Because I believe in love at first site.

❖

Imagination is the highest kite that one can fly.

❖

'**D**aughter,' said the suspicious father, 'that young man who's been walking with you through the park, strikes me as being exceedingly unpolished.'

'Well,' she answered coyly, 'he's a little rough around the hedges.'

❖

When one of the two first-grade teachers at the posh suburb's new school left on her two-week honeymoon, the other volunteered to teach both classes in her absence. A few weeks later, at a house-warming party given by the newly-weds, the guests were somewhat taken aback as the groom introduced them to his wife's teaching colleague: 'And this, ladies and gentlemen,' announced the grateful husband, 'is the lovely lady who substituted for my wife during our honeymoon.'

❖

Originally scheduled for all-night duty at the station, Patrolman Michael Fenwick was relieved early, and thus arrived home four hours ahead of schedule. It was nearly two a.m., and hoping to get into bed without waking his wife, he decided to undress in the dark. But as he crossed the room to climb into bed, his wife sat up and sleepily asked, 'Mike, dearest, would you go down to the all-night drugstore in the next block and get me a box of aspirin? My head is splitting.'

'Certainly, sweetheart,' he said, and feeling his way across the room he crawled back into his clothes, and stumbled out of the house and down the street to the drugstore. As he arrived, the pharmacist looked up in surprise.

'Say,' said the druggist, after taking Fenwick's order, 'aren't you Officer Fenwick of the Ninth Precinct?'

'Yes, I am,' said Fenwick.

'Well, then, what in the world are you doing in the fire chief's uniform?'

❖

A beachcomber of twenty-five had been shipwrecked on a desert island since the age of six. One day, while in search of food, he stumbled across a beautifully sensuous female lying on the beach nearly naked; she had been washed ashore from another shipwreck just that morning. After they got over their initial surprise at seeing each other, the girl wanted to know how long he had been alone there.

'Almost twenty years,' he said.

'Twenty years,' she exclaimed. 'But however did you survive?'

'Oh, I fish, dig for clams, and gather berries and coconuts,' he replied.

'And what do you do for sex?' she

asked.

'What's that?' he looked puzzled.

Whereupon the bold maiden pulled the innocent beachcomber down onto the sand beside her and proceeded to demonstrate. After they had finished, she asked how he had enjoyed it.

'Great,' was the reply. 'But look what it did to my clam-digger!'

❖

Harry constantly irritated his friends with his eternal optimism. No matter how bad the situation, he would always say, 'It could have been worse.'

To cure him of his annoying habit, his friends decided to invent a situation so completely black, so dreadful, that even Harry could find no hope in it. Approaching him at the club bar one day, one of them said, 'Harry! Did you hear what happened to George? He came home last night, found his wife in bed with another man, shot them both, then turned the gun on himself!'

'Terrible,' said Harry. 'But it could have been worse.'

'How in hell,' asked his dumbfounded friend, 'could it possibly have been worse?'

'Well,' said Harry, 'if it had happened the night before, I'd be dead now.'

❖

'My wife is always asking for money,' complained a friend of ours. 'Last week she wanted two hundred dollars. The day before yesterday she asked me for one hundred and twenty-five dollars. This morning she wanted one hundred and fifty dollars.'

'That's crazy,' we said. 'What does she do with it all?'

'I don't know,' said our friend. 'I never give her any.'

❖

Two successful business executives met

at a trade convention.

'Tell me,' said one, 'how's business?'

'Well, you know how it is,' replied the other. 'My line is like sex. When it's good, it's wonderful, and when it's bad, it's still pretty good!'

❖

A young man approached his family physician and said, 'Doc, I'm afraid you'll have to remove my wife's tonsils one of these days.'

'My good man,' replied the doctor, 'I removed them six years ago. Did you ever hear of a woman having two sets of tonsils?'

'No,' the husband retorted, 'but you've heard of a man having two wives, haven't you?'

❖

The proof that women are all alike is that every one of them thinks she's different.

The well-stacked redhead stormed into police headquarters and shouted at the desk sergeant that a man had grabbed and kissed her while she was walking through the park.

'What did he look like?' the desk sergeant asked.

'I really don't know,' the girl replied.

'Lady, it's the middle of the afternoon on a clear, sunny day,' the sergeant said in an exasperated voice. 'How could a man grab and kiss you without you seeing what he looked like?'

'Well,' the redhead answered, 'for one thing, I always close my eyes when I'm being kissed.'

❖

The pretty young schoolteacher was concerned about one of her eleven-year-old students. Taking him aside after class one day, she asked. 'Victor, why has your schoolwork been so poor lately?'

'I can't concentrate,' replied the lad,

'I am afraid I've fallen in love.'

'Is that so?' said the teacher, holding back an urge to smile. 'And with whom?'

'With you,' he answered.

'But Victor,' exclaimed the secretly pleased young lady, 'don't you see how silly that is? It's true that I would like a husband of my own someday; but I don't want a child.'

'Oh, don't worry,' said Victor reassuringly. 'I'll be careful.'

❖

'Though there are two dozen houses of ill fame in our town,' said the candidate for mayor to his attentive audience at the political rally, 'I have never gone to one of them.'

From the back of the crowd a heckler called out, 'Which one?'

❖

The TV quiz show anchor was

interviewing a pair of newlyweds.

'So you've only been married six days?' he cried.

'That's right!' the pretty bride replied hastily. 'But it seems like six months!'

'How is that?' the anchor boomed jovially.

'Well,' the girl answered thoughtfully, 'I guess it's because we've done so much in such a short time.'

❖

His last will and testament completed, the old man in the oxygen tent fondly told his son that all his wealth, stocks, bonds, bank account and real estate would be his after the end finally came.

'Dad, Dad,' whispered the weeping son, his voice emotion-choked, 'I can't tell you how grateful I am, how unworthy I am! Is there anything I can do for you? Anything at all?'

'Well, son,' came the feeble reply, 'I'd appreciate it very much if you took your foot off the oxygen hose.'

❖

A sexy blonde with a stunning figure boarded a bus and, finding no vacant seats, asked a gentleman for his, explaining that she was pregnant. The man stood up at once and gave her his seat, but couldn't help commenting that she didn't look pregnant.

'Well,' she replied with a smile, 'It's only been about half an hour.'

❖

After rushing into a drugstore, the nervous young man was obviously embarrassed when a prim middle-aged woman asked if she could serve him.

'N-no,' he stammered. 'I'd much rather see the druggist.'

'I'm the druggist,' she responded cheerfully. 'What can I do for you?'

'Oh well, uh, it's nothing important,' he said, and turned to leave.

'Young man,' said the woman, 'my sister and I have been running this drugstore for nearly thirty years. There is nothing you can tell us that will embarrass us.'

'Well, all right,' he said. 'I have this awful sexual hunger that nothing will appease. No matter how many times I make love. I still want to make love again and again. Is there anything you can give me for it?'

'Just a moment,' said the little lady. 'I'll have to discuss this with my sister.'

A few minutes later she returned. 'The best we can offer,' she said, 'is two hundred dollars a week and a half-interest in the business.'

❖

In keeping with all self-respecting vehicles owned by travelling salesmen,

Ed's car broke down in the middle of a blizzard, and he trudged to a nearby farmhouse. The farmer, being up in his lines, said: 'We're short of beds, but you can sleep with my daughter.' She proved to be sixteen, doe-eyed, with a strapping figure of healthy young womanhood. So they went to bed. And shortly, Ed made a pass at the daughter.

'Stop that!' she said. 'I'll call my father.' He desisted. But half an hour later he made another attempt.

'Uh. . .stop that.' she said 'I'll call my father.' But she moved closer to him, so he made a third try. This time, no protest, no threat. Just as Ed, satisfied, was about to drowse off, she tugged at his pajama sleeve.

'Could we do that again?' she asked. Ed obliged, and this time fell asleep, only to be awakened by the tug at his sleeve.

'Again?' And again Ed obliged. But when his sleep was once more rudely interrupted by the tugging at his pajama sleeve, Ed indignantly pulled it away from her and mumbled, 'Stop that! Or I'll call your father.'

❖

Art is the demonstration that the ordinary is extraordinary.

❖

The editor of a small weekly newspaper, in a rage over several government bills that had recently been passed, ran a scathing editorial under the headline: HALF OF OUR LEGISLATORS ARE CROOKS. Many prominent local politicians were outraged, and tremendous pressure was exerted on him to retract the statement. He finally succumbed to the pressure and ran an apology with the headline: HALF OF OUR LEGISLATORS ARE NOT CROOKS.

❖

Homer and his pretty wife were about to check out of the hotel, when Homer expostulated over the amount of the bill.

'But that, sir,' explained the hotel manager, 'is our normal rate for a double room with bath and TV.'

'Yeah? Well, as it happens, we didn't use the TV.'

'I'm sorry, sir. . .the manager replied firmly. 'It was there for you to use if you had wanted it.'

'That's okay,' Homer said, 'but in that case I am going to charge you for making love to my beautiful wife.'

'But, sir,' spluttered the manager. 'I did no such thing!'

'That's okay,' Homer said, 'she was there for you to use if you had wanted her.'

At this reply, the manager became so flustered that he actually reduced Homer's bill. Homer was exultant at his coup, and for months afterward he told and retold the story at parties with great relish, while his wife rolled her lovely eyes heavenward to indicate her opinion of his boorishness. Finally, they took another trip. Homer was determined to pull the same stunt and up to a point, he achieved the same success.

'Sir, that's our normal rate,' said the young clerk.

'Very well, but we didn't use the TV.'

'But, sir, it was there for you to use if you had cared to.'

Homer's eyes brightened in anticipation. 'Well, in that case,' he said. 'I'll have to charge you for making love to my beautiful wife.'

To Homer's chagrin, the clerk became very red in the face and began to stammer. Then he said. 'Okay, okay, I'll pay you. But keep your voice down, will you? I'm new at this hotel and you're apt to get me fired.'

❖

A ninety-year-old man who tried to

seduce a fifteen-year girl was charged with assault with a dead weapon.

A business executive on an out-of-town sales trip was about to check in at a hotel when he noticed a lusciously proportioned young woman smiling at him provocatively. Very casually, he walked over to her and spoke a few inaudible words. He returned to the desk with her clinging to his arm and they registered as man and wife. After a two-day stay, he checked out and was handed an astronomical bill.

'There's some mistake here,' he protested. 'I've only been here two days.'

'Yes.' the clerk explained, 'but your wife has been here for two months.'

❖

The cute and efficient young maid seemed to enjoy her work until one day, without warning, she gave notice.

'Why do you wish to leave?' the lady

of the house asked her. 'Is there anything wrong?'

'I just can't stand the suspense in this house a minute more,' the maid replied.

'Suspense,' said the confused mistress. 'What do you mean?'

'It's the sign over my bed,' the girl explained. 'You know, the one that says: WATCH YE, FOR YE KNOW NOT WHEN THE MASTER COMETH.'

❖

The old maid rushed up to the policeman. 'I've been raped. I've been attacked,' she cried. 'He ripped off my clothing. He smothered me with burning kisses. Then he made mad, passionate love to me!'

'Calm yourself, calm yourself, madam,' said the officer. 'Just when did all this take place?'

'Twenty-three years ago this September', said the woman.

'Twenty-three years ago!' he exclaimed. 'How do you expect me to arrest anyone for something he did twenty-three years ago?'

'Ah, I don't want you to arrest anyone, Officer,' said the woman. 'I just like to talk about it, that's all.'

❖

He held her close against himself, a warm glow of satisfaction covering them both.

'Am I the first man you ever made love to?' he asked.

She studied him reflectively. 'You might be,' she said. 'Your face looks very familiar.'

❖

The divorce court was attentive as the wealthy woman complained to the judge that her husband had left her bed and board. When she had finished, the husband rose to his feet and coolly replied, 'A slight correction, Your Honour. I left her bed-bored.'

❖

It was the young Englishman's first visit to the States, and in his innocence he sought lodging in the city's red-light district. His money, however, was as green as his outlook and the madam gladly offered him a room for the night. When a friend questioned him about his accommodations over lunch the following day, the young Briton replied:

'Well, the room wasn't very pretentious, you know, but God, what maid service!'

❖

Our unabashed dictionary defines old age as a time, when a man sees a pretty girl and it arouses his memory instead of his hopes.

❖

Mike had just moved into his apartment and decided he should get acquainted with his across-the-hall neighbour. When the door was opened, he was pleasantly surprised to be confronted by a young damsel considerably more than passing fair and considerably less than fully clad. Though justifiably flustered by this smiling apparition, Mike nevertheless managed a remark singularly appropriate to the occasion.

'Hi, I'm your new sugar across the hall—can I borrow a cup of neighbour?'

❖

A travelling salesman whose car broke down in a rainstorm, ran to the closest farmhouse and knocked on the door. A grizzled old farmer answered, and the salesman pleaded for a place to stay the night.

'I can give ya a room,' said the farmer, 'but I ain't got no daughter for ya to sleep with.'

'Oh!' said the salesman. 'Well, how far is it to the next house?'

❖

The meek little bank clerk had his suspicions. One day he left work early, and sure enough, at home he found a strange hat and umbrella in the hallway, and his wife was on the couch in the living room in the arms of another man. Wild for revenge, the husband picked up the man's umbrella and snapped it in two across his knee.

'There!' he exclaimed. 'Now I hope it rains!'

❖

Interviewing the sixty-year-old rodeo champion in Amarillo, Texas, the New York newspaperman remarked, 'You're really an extraordinary man, to be a rodeo champion at your age.'

'Heck,' said the cowboy, 'I'm not nearly the man my pa is. He was just signed to play guard for a pro-football team, and he's eighty-eight.'

'Amazing!' gasped the journalist. 'I'd like to meet your father.'

'Can't right now. He's in Fort Worth standing up for grandpa. Grandpa is getting married tomorrow. He's a hundred and fourteen.'

'Your family is simply unbelievable,' said the newspaperman. 'Here you are, a rodeo champion at sixty-five. Your father's a football player at eighty-eight. And now your grandfather wants to get married at a hundred and fourteen.'

'Hell, mister, you got that wrong,' said the Texan. 'Grandpa doesn't *want* to get married. He *has* to.'

Joe sat at his dying wife's bedside. Her voice was little more than a whisper.

'Joe, darling,' she breathed. 'I've got a confession to make before I go . . . I . . . I'm the one who took the ten thousand dollars from your safe . . . I spent it on a fling with your best friend, Charles. And it was I who forced your mistress to leave the city. And I am the one who reported your income-tax evasion to the government . . .'

'That's all right, dearest, don't give it a second thought,' answered Joe. 'I'm the one who poisoned you.'

❖

George was describing his new secretary enthusiastically to the family at dinner: 'She's efficient, personable, clever, punctual and darned attractive to boot. In short, she's a real doll!'

'A doll?' said his wife.

'A doll!' re-emphasized George.

At which point their five-year-old daughter, who knew about dolls, looked up from her broccoli to ask, 'And does she close her eyes when you lay her down, daddy?'

❖

Joe had been out of the town with a dazzling blonde, and as he returned home, the rosy tints of dawn began to colour the skies. Marshalling his inner resources, he managed an air of quiet sobriety before the suspicious eye and clapping tongue of his wife.

Suddenly, as he was undressing, she punctuated her harangue with a sharp, gasping intake of air.

'Joe,' she asked through clenched teeth, 'where's your underwear?'

Blearily Joe perceived that his boxer shorts were, indeed, missing. Then inspiration struck.

'My God!' he cried with aggrieved

dignity. 'I've been robbed!'

❖

The moon shone silver on the waters of the lake, and the waves beating on the shore were hardly equal in intensity to the waves of passion nearby. One ardent couple pulled apart long enough for the young man to whisper, 'Darling, am I the first man to make love to you?'

Her tone, when she answered, was irritated. 'Of course you are,' she said. 'I don't know why you men always ask the same ridiculous question.'

❖

Barry had just opened his law office and immediately hired three good-looking young stenographers to work for him.

'But how,' a visiting friend inquired eyeing the three, 'do you expect to accomplish anything?'

'Simple,' Barry grinned. 'By giving two of them the day off.'

❖

The bountifully endowed young lady was in an embarrassing situation, for her arms were filled with packages and she was wearing a dress that was simply too tight to allow her to step up into the bus for which she had been waiting the last fifteen minutes. A crowd pressed from behind, and so she reached back, unobserved she hoped, and attempted to gain some additional freedom by pulling down the zipper at the back of her dress. It didn't seem to help. She still couldn't negotiate the high step; so she reached again for the zipper and additional freedom but again it was no use. Then, from out of the impatient crowd behind her, a young man picked her up and deposited her gently inside the bus.

This, of course, only embarrassed the

girl more. 'What right have you to pick me up like that?' she gasped. 'Why, I don't even know you!'

'Well, miss,' the man said, smiling and tipping his hat, 'after you pulled my zipper down the second time, I began to feel as though we were pretty good friends.'

❖

Getting married is a good deal like going into a restaurant with friends. You order what you want, then when you see what the other fellow has, you wish you had taken that.

❖

The announcements of the professor's new book on astrophysics and his wife's new baby appeared almost simultaneously in the newspaper. Upon being congratulated on 'this proud event in the family', the professor naturally thought of the achievement that had cost him the greater effort.

'Thank you,' he replied modestly, 'but I couldn't have done it without the help of two graduate students.'

❖

Roger, the handsome real-estate agent, couldn't remember when he had rented an apartment to a more desirable tenant. As she bent over his desk to sign the lease, he became aware that his pulse was beating in his ears with the sound of bongo drums.

'Well,' he said, 'that's that. I wish you much happiness in your new apartment and here are the two keys that come with it.'

She straightened up, accepted the keys and favoured him with a dazzling smile.

'And here is a month's rent in advance, honey,' she replied. And she handed him back one of the keys.

❖

The trouble with being the best man at a wedding is that you don't get a chance to prove it.

❖

While John's wife was in delivery at the Maternity hospital, he was in the waiting room: nervous, agitated, prespiring. He was about to become a father for the first time.

Also waiting was a neighbour of John named Mendal, but he was very nonchalant because he had been through this many times.

John spoke to the older man.

'Mendal, there's something worrying me. May be you can advise me because you have several children.'

'Okay, what's the trouble?'

'Well,' hesitated John, 'I've been wondering how soon after, er . . . how long do I have to wait . . . that is, when can my wife and I . . . you know what I mean.'

'Oh sure,' answered Mendal. 'Well, that depends whether your wife is in the ward or the private room.'

❖

She had been dating one man steadily for almost a year, and her mother was growing concerned.

'Exactly what are his intentions?'

'Well, mom, I'm really not sure,' Carol said. 'He's been keeping me pretty much in the dark.'

❖

She stood at the teller's window in the bank, a vision of desirable femininity marred only slightly by the fact that the light in her baby-blue eyes was more than somewhat vacant. The teller examined her and the cheque she wished to cash with equal concentration. Then he asked her if she could identify herself.

For a moment her lovely brows were corrugated by puzzlement, then, her expression brightening, she pulled a small mirror from her handbag, glanced at it and with relief, said, 'Yes, it's me, all right.'

❖

Over drinks, two animated gentlemen were having a rousing battle about the charms of a stunning actress of the silver screen.

'I say, she's overrated,' said one. 'Take away her eyes, her hair, her lips and her figure and what have you got?'

'My wife,' said the other with a heavy sigh.

❖

When a guy takes off his coat, he's not going to fight. When a guy takes off his wristwatch, watch out!

❖

Dexter had just returned from two weeks of vacation. He asked his boss for two more weeks off to get married.

'What!' shouted the boss. 'I can't give you more time now. Why didn't you get married while you were off?'

'Are you nuts?' replied Dexter. 'That would have ruined my entire vacation!'

❖

A woman writing at a post-office desk was approached by a man whose hand was in a cast. 'Pardon me,' said the man, 'but could you please address the post card for me?' The woman gladly did so, agreeing also to write a short message and sign for him.

'There,' said the woman, smiling. 'Is there anything else I can do for you?'

'Yes,' the man replied. 'At the end could you put 'PS—Please excuse the handwriting.'

❖

After they had brought their first baby home from the hospital, a young wife suggested to her husband that he try his hand at changing diapers. 'I'm busy,' he said. 'I'll do the next one.'

The next time the baby was wet, she asked if he was now ready to learn how to change diapers. He looked puzzled. 'Oh,' he replied finally. 'I didn't mean the next diaper. I meant the next baby!'

❖

Politicians are like diapers. They both should be changed often. And for the same reason.

One jogger, huffing and puffing, to another: 'The doctor told me jogging would add years to my life, and he certainly was right. I feel ten years older already.'

❖

As a salesman, Tom frequently visited a small New Zealand town. Once, he stayed at a hotel known for its appalling service. He made the mistake of ordering tea in bed. Shortly before seven a girl threw open the door. 'Sugar in your tea?' she shouted. 'No, thank you,' he replied. As she banged the door shut she said, 'Ah, well, don't stir it then.'

❖

Boss to employee: 'We've decided, Mohan, to give you more responsibility. From now on, you'll be responsible for everything that goes wrong.'

❖

John was in a shop waiting for his wife to try on a dress, and he exchanged a few remarks with a man standing nearby. Just then, the man's wife came up, shiny-eyed, obviously pleased with the dress she was wearing, but her husband shook his head negatively, saying he didn't like it. She was disappointed, but she didn't want to buy it if he didn't approve. She returned to the fitting room. He promptly asked the clerk the price of the dress, paid for it, asked that it be gift-wrapped and said he would pick it up later that afternoon.

Turning to John, he explained, 'Tomorrow is her birthday, and this is the only way I can surprise her with a new dress that she really likes.'

❖

In the steel township, there is a social club which, among other activities, screens a feature film every week for its members. The club's telephone number and Peter's home phone number are identical except for a slight change in the sequence of the digits. Naturally, on the day of the film show he is inundated with phone calls from people anxious to know what film is being screened and it tries his patience explaining that they've got the wrong number.

One Saturday evening, having answered a particularly large quota of misdialled numbers, he was straining to contain his irritation when the phone rang again for the umpteenth time. A booming voice demanded. 'What picture is being shown today?'

'Wrong number,' Peter said severely.

However, this time, instead of the usual apology, the caller shot back another question: 'Is it in English?'

❖

An investigator with a curious mind and a special device to measure temperature swears he has established these standards: cool as a cucumber, 20.5 degrees; warm as toast, 75 degrees; hot news, 32.7 degrees for front pages; cold shoulder given by a fashion model, 35.4 degrees; red pepper, 20.5 degrees before eating; and a pretty girl's kiss 33.3 degrees registered outdoors on a mild day.

❖

The Duke of Gloucester, speaking at a luncheon in London: 'A home accidents survey which showed that ninety percent of accidents on staircases involved either the top or the bottom step, was fed into a computer. Asked how accidents could be reduced, the computer answered : "Remove the top and bottom steps."'

❖

Like every other national leader, US president William Howard Taft had to endure his share of abuse. One night at the dinner table, his youngest boy made a disrespectful remark to him. There was a sudden hush. Taft looked thoughtful.

'Well,' said Mrs Taft, 'aren't you going to punish him?'

'If the remark was addressed to me as his father, he certainly will be punished,' said Taft. 'However, if he addressed it to the President of the United States, that is his constitutional privilege.'

❖

A small Indian boy appeared in the class of a London schoolteacher for the first time and she asked him his name. 'Venkataratnam Narasimha Rattaiah,' he said. When she asked, 'How do you spell it?' he replied, 'My mother helps me.'

❖

At a motor show, two car manufacturers

were talking about the latest improvements in their factories. 'In our place,' one of them said, 'we allocate crores to the construction of an industrial complex with test tracks designed to put our latest models through every possible and imaginable treatment.'

'I do the same thing a lot cheaper,' said the other. 'When we bring out a new model, I lend it to my son for the week-end.'

❖

On a geography field trip, a friend pointed to some cows. 'It's going to rain,' he said. 'They say that if cows are lying down, it means rain, and if they are standing up, it will be dry.'

A little later they saw more cows, some lying down and others standing. When asked, the friend gave his latest weather forecast. He paused only a moment, then declared confidently: 'Scattered showers!'

It's sad for a girl to reach the age
Where men consider her charmless.
But it's worse for a man to attain the age
Where the girls consider him harmless.

❖

The nurse motioned to one of the expectant fathers and announced, 'You have a son.' Another man dropped his cigarette, jumped up and cried, 'Say, what's the idea? I was here before he was.'

❖

A young soldier who was on a twenty-four-hour pass went to a dance in town and there met an atrractive cutie. As they danced, he romanced her. Finally, he gasped, 'Look sweetheart, I really go for you in a big way. But I don't have much time. I have to be back in the morning. I'd sure like to speed things up between us.'

She stared wide-eyed at him and said,

'I am dancing as fast as I can.'

❖

A woman tourist stranded in the hills of Kentucky during a severe electrical storm sought shelter at a small shack nearby. An aged man welcomed her and told her that she might sleep there if she didn't mind sleeping with grandpa.

The tourist had no objection and soon turned in. In the morning she thanked the old man profusely and told him that grandpa had not disturbed her one bit. The old man replied, 'Well, he shouldn't ought to, he's been dead five days.'

❖

The queen was travelling in the back country when she chanced to meet a man, his wife and a flock of children. Impressed, the queen asked: 'Are all of these your children?'

'Yes, your Highness,' answered the man.

'How many children do you have?' questioned the queen.

'Sixteen,' was the reply.

'Sixteen children,' repeated the queen. 'We should give you a knighthood.'

'He has one,' piped up the lady, 'but he won't wear it.'

❖

A young husband watched his flat-chested wife as she tried on her new brassiere.

'What did you buy that for?' he asked. 'You haven't got anything to put in it.'

'You wear shorts don't you?' she retorted.

❖

Dr Feels turned to Joe. 'You won't live a week if you don't stop running around with women.'

Joe pounded his chest a la Tarzan. 'Why, there's nothing the matter with me. I'm in great physical shape.'

Dr Feels retorted, 'Yes, I know. But one of the women is my wife.'

❖

A tiny tot sought admission to the junior branch of a school on the strength of having an elder brother in the final year class in the same school. The elder brother had described the aspirant as his 'real brother'. When the little fellow appeared before the Interview Board and was questioned about the relationship, he replied, 'He is a distant relative.'

'How come you call him a distant relative when he says you are his real brother?' asked the Principal.

'Sir, there are nine brothers and sisters between him and me.'

❖

An assistant on the lingerie counter of a chain store was at a loss for words when one woman handed her a paper bag and said, 'I'm afraid this brassiere doesn't fit. Could I exchange it for two pillow cases?'

❖

When a London landlord wrote to one of his tenants, giving him a month's notice, he received the most courteous of brief replies. 'Dear sir,' it read, 'I remain, Yours faithfully . . .'

❖

A policeman stopped a motorist at night and pointed out that a front light was not working. The driver got out to have a look, kicked the car, and the light came on. 'There you are,' he said smugly. 'It only needed a kick.'

'Try kicking the windshield,' replied the policeman, 'your inspection sticker is also out of date.'

❖

The patient looks distrustfully at his prescription, then at the doctor and says, 'In my state of depression, I need something to stimulate me. Something that excites me, that challenges me, that works me up. Is there anything like that in this prescription?'

'Nope,' says the doctor. 'You'll find that in the bill.'

❖

From what we get, we can make a living; what we give, however, makes a life.

❖

A doctor came into a hospital room and told the patient's husband to wait outside while he examined his wife. A few minutes later, the doctor came out and asked a nurse if she could get him a pair of pliers. She did, and he went back into the patient's room. Five minutes later he came out and asked for a screwdriver. When he came out a third time and asked for a hammer, the anxious husband demanded to know what was wrong with his wife. 'I don't know yet,' the doctor said. 'I can't get my bag open.'

❖

A woman visited the bank to close her account because she was convinced the institution was going under. Asked by a startled manager why she thought so, she produced one of her cheques endorsed by the bank with the legend 'insufficient funds'.

❖

On a hot summer day an elderly

gentleman faints in the street. A small crowd immediately gathers around him.

'Give the poor man a glass of brandy,' advises a woman.

'Take his pulse first,' someone else suggests.

'No, just give him some brandy,' insists the woman.

'Call an ambulance,' yells another person.

'A brandy!'

The man suddenly sits up and exclaims, 'Shut up, everybody, and do as the kind lady says!'

❖

A physician told me about one of his favourite patients. The doctor once asked the fellow if he had lived in the same place all his life. The man replied. 'Nope, I was born in the bedroom next to the one where I sleep now.'

❖

Driving late one night, the husband and wife were feeling a bit amorous, so they stopped at a secluded spot. Soon after, a police officer pulled up and asked to see their drivers' licences. 'I don't believe it,' he said, 'you're married!'

❖

Solitude is a good place to visit but a poor place to stay.

❖

Susan was celebrating her fifth wedding anniversary, and her father and mother racked their brains to think of an appropriate gift. Knowing she and her husband would appreciate a joke, they bought them a wooden stepladder which would also be practical. On the way to deliver it they stopped for petrol. The young attendant, seeing the ladder with card and large pink bow attached, asked 'What's that about?'

'It's a gift for our daughter,' the father replied.

He grinned, 'You are hoping she'll elope?'

❖

'**I**'m so depressed that girls refuse to date with me because of my weight,' the hundred-and thirty-five-kilos weighing man told the priest. 'I've tried everything to lose weight but in vain.'

'I think I can help,' said the priest. 'Tomorrow, be ready to go out at 8 a.m.'

Next morning, a beautiful woman in a skin-tight exercise suit knocked on the man's door. 'If you can catch me, you can have me,' she said, as she took off. He huffed and puffed after her.

This routine went on every day for the next five months. The man lost more than 50 kilos and felt confident that he would catch the woman the next day. That morning he whipped open his front door and found a hundred-and-thirty-five kilo woman in a jogging suit waiting for him. 'The priest said to tell you,' she began, 'that if I can catch you, I can have you.'

❖

Wife: There's trouble with the car. It has water in the carburettor.

Husband: Water in the carburettor? That's ridiculous.

Wife: I tell you the car has water in the carburettor.

Husband: You don't even know what a carburettor is. Where's the car?

Wife : In the swimming pool.

❖

'**H**ow's the new patient feeling?' the doctor asked the nurse.

'Oh, he's much better,' she replied. 'He started talking this morning.'

'What did he say?'

'He said he was feeling much worse.'

❖

While driving his nine-year-old to elementary school, Dad asked him which high school he'd like to attend. He reminded Dad he was only in the fourth standard. Dad then asked what college he planned to attend. Getting annoyed, he said he didn't know. A minute later he said he wanted to pose a question to Dad. 'Fine,' Dad replied.

'Dad,' he asked, 'what cemetery would you like to be buried in?'

❖

A man went into a pub and ordered six whiskies. Lining them up on the bar he downed the first glass then the third and finally the fifth.

'Excuse me,' said the barman as the man turned to leave. 'But you've left three glasses untouched.'

'Yes, I know,' said the man. 'My doctor said it was okay to take the odd drink.'

❖

Happiness is a thing to be practised, like the violin.

❖

There was a political leader who was on the verge of being defeated in the elections. When he received a phone call saying that his wife had delivered triplets, he exclaimed 'Oh, no! I demand a recount.'

❖

A man who had just died, arrived at heaven's gate. Before allowing him entry, St. Peter questioned him. 'Did you love a woman?'

'No,' the man replied, 'I never loved a

single one.'

'Did you have a friend you cared for?'

'No, I never cared for anyone.'

'Perhaps you loved a pet? Did you not feel a love for nature?'

'No.'

'What took you so long to get here?' a surprised St. Peter asked him. 'You've been dead for ages.'

❖

One morning Mike opened the door to get the newspaper and was surprised to see a strange little dog with his paper in its mouth. Delighted with this unexpected 'delivery service', he fed the dog some treats. The following morning he was horrified to see the same dog sitting in front of his door, wagging its tail, surrounded by as many as eight newspapers.

He spent the rest of that morning returning the papers to their owners.

On a crisp autumn afternoon the four-year-old son was helping his father rake leaves in the front yard of the farmhouse. The child glanced up just in time to see a flock of geese flying over and pointed out how they flew in a formation shaped like the letter 'V'.

He patiently watched them as they disappeared over the horizon and then turning to his father asked, 'Do they know any other letters?'

❖

A three-year-old boy went with his dad to see a new litter of kittens. On returning home, he breathlessly informed his mother, 'There were two boy kittens and two girl kittens.'

'How did you know that?' his mother asked.

'Daddy picked them up and looked underneath,' he replied. 'I think it's printed on the bottom.'

❖

Husband and wife had just finished tucking the four young ones into bed one evening when they heard sounds of sobbing coming from three-year-old Eric's room. Rushing to his side, they found him crying hysterically. He had accidentally swallowed a penny and was sure he was going to die. No amount of reassurances to the contrary could change his mind.

Desperate to calm him, the husband secretly put a penny that he happened to have in his pocket into his hand and pretended to pull it from Eric's ear. Eric was delighted. In a flash, he snatched it from the husband's hand, swallowed it and demanded cheerfully, 'Do it again, Dad!'

❖

The young man, a very bright sixteen-year-old, was halfway through his first year at university when his grandfather came to visit.

'How's the work going,' Grandfather asked.

'Fine,' was the reply.

'And the social life?'

'I get lots of dates,' replied the young man, 'if I don't tell the girls my age.'

'I understand,' said the youthful-looking seventy-year-old widower. 'I have the same problem.'

❖

A balloonist landed in a field and, realizing he was lost, asked a passerby where he was.

'You're in the middle of a field in a hot-air balloon.'

'You must be an accountant,' said the balloonist.

'How did you know that?'

'Because your information is totally accurate and absolutely useless.'

❖

Question: Why do some testing labs prefer to use lawyers instead of mice? Answer: Because there are more lawyers than mice, the scientists don't get as attached to the lawyers, and there are some things mice won't do.

❖

Kissing: A means of getting two people so close together that they can't see anything wrong with each other.

❖

My sister-in-law, a prospective juror, was asked by the trial judge if she belonged to any secret societies. She replied that she did, but would not tell him which one.

The judge explained that she must answer the question fully, but again she adamantly refused.

Exasperated, he said, 'Young lady, I

am going to ask you one more time and if you refuse, I will hold you for contempt of court!'

'All right, Your Honour,' she confessed. 'I belong to Overeaters Anonymous.'

❖

The teenage grandson was eager to get his first summer job at a bicycle rental shop. During his interview, he was asked, 'How are you at handling irate customers?'

'I haven't had experience with irate customers,' he replied, 'but I'm pretty good with irate parents.'

He got the job.

❖

Lawyer: You say you want a divorce because your husband is careless about his appearance?

Wife: Yes. He hasn't shown up in two years.

Our son asked if he could borrow some money to buy a car. The father explained that borrowing money is a bad habit. 'Son, I got my first motorcycle when I was nineteen, and with my own money. I got my first car at twenty-four, and with my own money. And I got my second car when I got married, and with my own money.'

At this point the son interjected excitedly, 'So there is no problem. This car would be with your own money as well.'

❖

If laughter could be ordered by prescription, then every doctor would certainly prescribe it. Not mere snickers, but hearty chuckles and guffaws. It's an established fact that when you laugh your entire system gets a lift, and you can't laugh that off.

❖

A bachelor is a person who would rather have a woman on his mind than on his neck.

❖

A rather naive young man named Ram had recently reached manhood and had no idea why he was continuously nervous and tense. He went to see his doctor. The doctor was not in, but his nurse was a redheaded beauty who wore her uniform so tight that Ram's jitters noticeably increased. She asked him what was wrong, and he told her. She eyed him appraisingly.

'That's easy to fix,' she said. 'Come with me.' She led Ram into a small examination room and there relieved his tensions.

As he was preparing to leave, she said, 'That will be twenty dollars.' And, quite satisfied, Ram was pleased to pay.

Several weeks went by and Ram

found the same unrest growing in him again. He returned to the doctor's office, and this time the doctor was in. He listened to Ram's symptoms, then wrote out a prescription on a piece of paper and handed it to him.

'This is for tranquilizers,' the doctor said. 'You can have it filled downstairs. That will be five dollars, please.'

Ram looked at the small piece of paper for a few moments, then looked up at the doctor and said, 'If it's all the same to you, Doc, I'd just as soon have the twenty-dollar treatment.'

❖

A man was travelling in a train, and noticed that his seat number was 77, in the seventh compartment. His ticket was numbered 777. The train terminated at platform number seven, and his taxi happened to have the number 7777. His hotel room, on the seventh floor, was

172 The Funniest Jokes in the World

number 77. So, he thought, 'There is something in all this.' The town he was visiting was famous for its horse races, and, therefore, reading a message from fate, he went to the race track and placed a heavy bet on horse number seven.

Eagerly, he awaited the results of the race, almost certain that the number seven would work its magic. Well, it did in a way. That horse finished seventh.

❖

A woman was in a modern art studio trying to decide what to buy. She was having a tough time. Finally she picked out one frame and looked it up and down, this way and that.

Then she called out to the salesman. 'I cannot figure out which is the top and which is the bottom,' she fumed. 'Is this what you call modern art?'

The salesman looked sheepish. 'No madam,' he replied, 'this is not modern art. This is a looking glass. A mirror!'

❖

A young couple agreed that if either of them were to die, the surviving one would try to make contact with the dead one exactly one year after the death. The wife was killed in an automobile accident. As arranged, he tried to make contact with her exactly one year later and succeeded. This is how the conversation went:

He: How are things?

She: Oh, things are just beautiful. We get up every morning and make love. We then eat breakfast and make love some more. After lunch, we usually take a nap and make love till supper, then make love some more until we go to sleep. Then the next morning we start all over again.

He: That is wonderful. I didn't know heaven would be like that.

She: I'm not in heaven. I'm a jack rabbit in Arizona.

The forgetful professor had left his umbrella in his hotel room when checking out. He missed it on the way to the train station, and still having time to spare, he hurried back. He found the room and was about to ask a passing chambermaid to open it for him, when he became aware of voices within and realized that, in the brief time since his departure, the room had been let to new occupants.

'Whose little baby are you?' asked a youthful male voice from behind the door, and the question was followed by the sound of kisses and a girlish giggle.

'Your little baby,' said the youthful female voice.

'And whose little hands are these?' asked the boy.

'Your little hands,' responded the girl with more giggles of delight.

'And whose little knees . . .? And whose little . . .?'

'When you get to an umbrella,' said the professor through the door, 'it's mine!'

It seems that when the good Lord was making the world, he called Man aside and bestowed upon him twenty years of normal sex life. Man thought that was too little, but the Creator refused to budge.

The Lord called the monkey next and gave him also twenty years of good life. 'But I don't need twenty years, ten years is plenty,' the monkey said. Man spoke up, 'May I have the other ten years?' The monkey agreed.

Then the Lord called the lion and also gave him twenty years. The lion said ten would be enough, so again Man spoke up, 'May I have your other ten years?' The lion agreed.

Next came the donkey with the same results, giving ten of his twenty years to the Man.

This explains how Man has twenty years of normal sex life, ten years of monkeying around, ten years of lioning about, and ten years of making an ass of himself.

Girl's father: My daughter sings so well that you will forget to listen to tape-recorders and stereos after you hear her. She dances so superbly that once you see her dancing, you will stop watching TV and VCR. And she washes clothes better than any washing machine.

Boy's father: But I have already accepted your daughter's hand for my son. So why are you telling me all that?

Girl's father: So that you do not ask for these items as part of her dowry.

❖

In married life, office plays a very important role. In fact it is the place where you relax from your strenuous home life!

❖

Leola Starling of Ribrock, Tennessee, had a serious telephone problem. The brand new ten-million-dollar Ribrock Plaza Motel that opened nearby had acquired almost the same telephone number as Leola's. From the moment the motel opened, she was besieged with calls not for her. Since she had had the same phone number for years, she tried to persuade the motel management to change its number, but they refused, claiming that the motel could not change its stationery. The phone company was not helpful either.

After her pleas fell on deaf ears, Leola decided to take matters into her own hands.

At nine the phone rang. Someone from Memphis was calling the motel and asked for a room the following Tuesday. Leola said: 'No problem. How many nights?'

Emboldened, Leola continued reserving rooms—the presidential suite (which was priced at six hundred dollars a night) was reserved without any deposit the next morning. She booked an electric appliance manufacturers' convention for Memorial Day weekend, a college prom and a reunion of the 82nd Airborne Veterans from World War II. But her biggest challenge came in the afternoon when a mother called to book the ballroom for her daughter's wedding in June. Leola assured the woman that it would be no problem and even committed that the motel would take care of the floral arrangement and would not charge for valet parking.

Within a few months, the Ribrock Plaza Motel was a disaster area. People kept showing up for weddings, bar dances and sweet sixteen parties, and were all told there were no such events.

Leola had her final revenge when she read in the papers that the motel might go bankrupt. Her phone rang, and an executive from Marriot said: 'We're prepared to offer you two hundred thousand dollars for the motel.'

Leola said: 'I'll take it, but only if you change the telephone number.'

❖

Newton Hooton gets up one morning, walks into the bathroom, turns on the tap, but it does not work. So he calls out to his wife, Helen Hooton, in the bedroom, 'Hey honey, the water tap doesn't work!'

'Well, Sweetie,' calls back Helen, 'you are the man in the house—you fix it!'

'Hey, I'm no plumber,' replies Newton. Then he goes over to the clothes closet to get his suit, and the door handle comes off in his hand.

'Hey, Helen,' shouts Newton, 'the closet door handle is broken!'

'Well, darling, you are the man in the house,' shouts back Helen. 'You fix it!'

'Hey, I'm no carpenter!' snaps Newton, and he goes downstairs for his breakfast. But when he switches on the light in the kitchen, the bulb pops.

'Hey, honey,' shouts out Newton. 'The light is busted!'

'Well, sugar-pie,' calls back Helen, 'why don't you fix it?'

'Hey, I'm no electrician,' shouts back Newton, and he goes off to work.

That evening, Newton comes home and sees a new light bulb in the kitchen. He goes upstairs, and the door handle on the closet is fixed. Then he goes into the bathroom, and the water tap works. 'Hey, honey,' shouts out Newton. 'Who fixed all these broken things in the house?'

'Well, baby-cakes,' calls back Helen, 'Burton Belch from next door must have heard us shouting this morning, so he came over and offered to fix everything.'

'That's great, honey,' shouts Newton. 'But what did he want in payment?'

'Well dearie,' replies Helen, 'he said I could either please him or bake him a cake.'

'Hey, honey,' shouts Newton, 'that is nice. What kind of cake did you bake him?'

'Hey, poopsie,' calls out Helen, 'I'm no baker!'

❖

Little Ernie is doing his homework one evening and has a problem.

'Dad,' he says, 'What is the difference between "anger" and "exasperation"?'

'Well, son,' says his father, 'I will give you a practical demonstration.'

His father then goes to the phone and dials a random number.

'Hello,' comes a voice at the other end.

'Hello,' says Ernie's father. 'Is Melvin there?'

'There is no one called Melvin here!' comes the reply. 'Why don't you learn to look up numbers before you dial them?'

'You see?' says Ernie's father. 'That man was not at all happy with our call. But watch this!'

He then dials the same number again, and says, 'Hello, is Melvin there?'

'Now look here!' comes the angry reply. 'I told you there is no Melvin here! You have got a lot of nerve calling again!' And then he slams down the receiver.

'Did you hear that?' asks Ernie's father. 'That was "anger". Now, I will show you what "exasperation" is!'

He picks up the phone and dials the same number again, and when a violent voice shouts, 'Hello!' Ernie's father says, 'Hello! This is Melvin. Have there been any calls for me?'

❖

'Some young man is trying to get into my room through the window,' screamed the lady into the telephone.

'Sorry, lady,' came back the answer, 'You've got the fire department. What you want is the police department.'

'No, no,' she pleaded, 'I want the fire department. What he needs is a longer ladder to come into the room!'

'My poor husband,' said the lady to her psychoanalyst, dragging her husband behind her. 'He's convinced he's a parking meter.'

The analyst looked at the silent, morbid fellow and asked, 'Why doesn't he say something for himself? Can't he talk?'

'How can he,' said the lady, 'with all those coins in his mouth?'

❖

This anecdote is about political parties employing goondas to rig polls. The goonda fraternity had its own undercover identification to establish its political credentials. The police got a wind of it. So when it arrested four hoodlums they were ordered to stand in line.

'Raise your *dhoti*,' ordered the police officer. The first man had a red *langoti*. 'Lock him up, he is communist,' ordered the official. The second wore a green *langoti*. 'Lock him up, he is a Majlis

Ittehad-e-Musalmeen.' The third had on a saffron underwear. 'Lock him up, he is BJP.' The fourth who didn't have any underwear, explained his nudity as 'an independent without political affiliations'. He was set free.

Moral: Do not wear *langoti* till the elections are over.

❖

A poor man sat outside a temple begging for alms from the devotees: 'In the name of Bhagwan give this hungry man some paise to fill his belly. Bhagwan will bless you.' But the people who went to pray in the temple, gave the poor beggar so little that it was never enough to buy *dal-roti*. In sheer disgust he quit the temple and sat outside a *theka* (a country liquor shop) where people came for their evening quota of *desi*. 'A few paise in the name of Bhagwan,' he whined, as people came out in high spirits. Instead of paise many dropped rupee notes in his begging bowl. The beggar gave thanks to God in the following words: 'Hey Bhagwan, truly inscrutable are thy ways! You give one address but live in another place.'

❖

The small boy asks, 'Daddy, are you still growing?'

'No, son, what makes you think so?'

'Because the top of your head is coming through your hair.'

❖

Sixty is a good age for a man. If she says yes, he is flattered. If she says no, he is relieved.

❖

Husband to wife as they emerge from a long session with a marriage guidance counsellor: 'Darling, I do love you.'

'There you go again,' snapped his wife. 'Hardly we come out of the place and it's I . . . I . . . I . . . always I . . .'

❖

'I had a terrible row with my wife last night over her buying a fur coat,' a man told his friend. 'But I had the final word.'

'What did you say?' the friend asked.

I said, 'Go and buy it.'

❖

'Listen,' shouted a big man through the telephone box to a little man inside, 'You've been holding that phone for nearly twenty-five minutes and not said a single word.'

'Sir,' said the little man, 'I'm talking to my wife!'

❖

Husband: What is this small parcel for, dear?
Wife: A bottle of hair tonic.
Husband: Thanks, dear.
Wife: It's for your typist. Her hair shows up badly on your coat!

❖

'**T**hey tell me that your son in college is quite an author. Does he write for money?'
'Yes, in every letter.'

❖

Two friends met in the street one day. 'Well,' said one, 'So you're married at last. My congratulations. I heard you have an excellent and accomplished wife.'

'I do, indeed,' was the reply. 'Why she's perfectly at home in science, in arts, in commerce, in short, she's at home everywhere, except . . .'

'Except what?' questioned his friend.

'Except at home,' was the reply.

❖

A: Please define a baby.
B: A baby is the most expensive employer of the female labour.

❖

'**D**arling, you are the most beautiful woman in the world.'
    'Oh, dear, how quick you are at noticing things!'

❖

Before marriage, when a man holds a girl's hand it is love; after marriage, it is self-defence.

❖

One smart husband on being charged

by his wife of forgetting her birthday said to the wife: 'How can you expect me to remember your birthday dear, when you never look any older?'

❖

The students of a college during the first year were often required to rise in class and say what their University meant to them. One day, a student rose to his feet and announced, rather nervously: 'My brother and I owe a lot to this University. You see, our parents met here!'

❖

'Are you saving any money by keeping a budget?'

'Sure, my wife and I are so serious about it that we have to stay in every evening to balance it. Then one things leads to another and it is too late to go anywhere!'

During a domestic quarrel the husband hid himself under a bed. At last the wife found him out. She asked him to come out. To this he replied: 'I am not afraid of you. After all I am a man. If I say I won't come out, I won't.'

❖

Annoyed wife to husband: 'Can't you just say we've been married twenty-four years instead of "almost a quarter of a century"?'

❖

Before marriage he used to catch her in his arms. Now he catches her in his pockets!

❖

Two wealthy, fashionable city women were strolling through the park.

'Oh, look!' exclaimed one. 'What a lovely baby in the carriage!'

'It is,' said the other, and they walked over to it.

'Good gracious,' cried the first. 'What a strange coincidence, it's my baby!'

Surprised, her friend asked, 'Are you sure?'

'Positive, darling, I recognize the nurse.'

❖

'**M**y husband would never chase any woman,' Mrs X confided to her best friend. 'He's too fine, too decent, too old.'

❖

Little Munni: Auntie, why do you put that powder on your face?

Auntie: To make myself look pretty.

Little Munni: Then why doesn't it work?

❖

Two middle-aged women were browsing in a book shop.

'Here's a book on "How to Torture Your Husband",' said one.

'I don't need it,' said the other. 'I've my own system.'

❖

'Please tell me the best medium,' asked one businessman of his advertising expert, 'of reaching my goods to every married woman of this town.'

'It's very easy,' said the expert. 'Please address all your letters to the husbands and mark the envelopes "Private & Confidential".'

❖

'Doctor, my wife has lost her voice. What can I do about it?'

'Try getting home late some night.'

❖

An expectant lady ordered her tailor to prepare a dressing gown for her in a week. The tailor was unusually late. A beautiful baby was born to her. Next time, when she met the tailor she complained about his procrastination in these words: 'You're never prompt. My delivery was faster than yours!'

❖

She: Don't you think that a little common sense would prevent many divorces?
He: Why, I'm sure that it would keep people from getting married in the first place!

❖

A woman came home one day and asked her new maid: 'Did you clean out the refrigerator as I told you to?'

'Yes, madam,' the maid said. 'And everything was so delicious.'

She married him for better or worse—
better for her and worse for him.

❖

A certain wife was on a perpetual
clothes-buying spree with the result that
her husband was near destruction, trying
to keep all the bills paid.

'You shouldn't allow your wife to run
up big bills like that,' advised a friend.
'Why don't you put a stop to it?'

'It's much easier,' the husband
explained, 'to make arrangements with
my creditors than with my wife.'

❖

A man to his neighbour, 'It's my wife's
garden. I only do the digging, planting,
watering and weeding!'

❖

On his fiftieth wedding anniversary, Henry Ford was asked his formula for a successful married life. He replied that it was the same that made his car successful: Stick to one model.

❖

'Darling . . .' began a young wife, hesitatingly.

'Yes dear?' said her husband.

'I hardly know how to tell you.'

'Tell me what?'

'Th-that soon there will be a third sharing our little home.'

'Sweetheart! Are you sure?'

'Positive, dear. I had a letter from my mother this evening saying that she would be here next Friday.'

❖

Suman: Mother, do fairy tales always begin with 'Once upon a time. . .'

Mother: No, my dear, not always; sometimes they also begin with, 'My love, I'll be detained at the office till nine tonight; hence I'll come late . . .'

❖

A husband is one who lays down the law to his wife and then accepts all her amendments.

❖

A married man makes a very good salesman.'
    'How?'
    'Because he is used to taking orders.'

❖

'Oh we're happy,' insisted the husband. 'Of course, once in a while my wife throws things at me. But that doesn't change the situation one bit, because if she hits me, she's happy. And if she misses, I'm happy.'

❖

An elderly woman with a propensity for practical jokes sent a huge, beautifully wrapped package to a prospective bride, 'Wear this on your wedding night, and you are bound to thrill your husband.'

Eagerly and excitedly, the young lady unwrapped the exquisite package. There was nothing in it.

❖

Cajoling wife to her husband: 'Darling, will you lend me two hundred rupees and only give me a hundred out of them? Then you'll owe me hundred and I'll owe you hundred and we'll be straight.'

❖

A woman has seven ages: Baby, Child, Girl, Young Woman, Young Woman,

Young Woman and Young Woman.

❖

Two Hollywood stars met at a party. 'Darling!' exclaimed the first, 'Your husband looks wonderful tonight. I've never seen him so fit and well. Perhaps its the new suit . . .?'

'No, it's not the suit. It's a new wife.'

❖

In the middle of a dispute the husband said: 'Let's not quarrel, my dear, let's discuss the thing sensibly.'

'No,' said the angry wife, 'every time we discuss something sensibly, I lose!'

❖

A fellow confessed to a friend, 'I got married because I was tired of going to the laundry, eating in restaurants and wearing socks with holes.'

'Funny,' the friend replied, 'I got divorced for that reason.'

❖

A fellow just bought a car. His wife went with him on a few expeditions, and did not hesitate to criticize his driving.

'Hello, old man!' said a neighbour one evening. 'I see you've got a car. What do you get out of her?'

'About forty thousand words to the gallon,' answered the husband.

❖

Husband (driving his car past a farmer's pair of mules which happened to bray at that moment): 'Relatives of yours, I suppose.'

Wife, smiling sweetly: 'Yes, by matrimony.'

❖

A lot of men believe in long engagements because they think that young couples ought to be happy as long as possible!

❖

Office boy: Sorry madam, but the boss has gone to lunch with his wife.
Wife: O well . . . tell him his stenographer had called.

❖

The guest speaker concluded a long boring speech and the Committee Chairman handed him a cheque.

'No, no,' said the speaker, 'I wouldn't think of charging you, please contribute my honorarium to some worthy cause.'

'Would you mind if we put it in our club's special fund?' asked the Chairman.

'Of course not, what is the fund for?'

'To help us to get better speakers.'

❖

At a pharmacy, a woman wanted to use the infant scale to weigh the baby she held in her arms. The clerk complained that the device was out for repairs, but said he would estimate the infant's size by weighing the mother and baby together on the adult scale, then weighing the mother alone and subtracting the second amount from the first.

'It won't work,' countered the woman. 'I'm not the mother, I'm the grandmother.'

❖

The difference between a helping hand and an outstretched palm is a twist of the wrist.

❖

A man was met by St. Peter at the gates to Heaven. 'Name?' asked St. Peter, looking at a list.

'Simon Magnus,' replied the man.

'Strange,' said St. Peter, 'You're not

on the list. What job did you do on earth?'

'I was a scrap-metal dealer.'

St. Peter shook his head, 'I'll need higher authority for this,' he said, walking off through the magnificent gates. When he came back, the gates were gone.

❖

While visiting relatives, Ram noticed that they had replaced their usual TV with a smaller model. Thinking that perhaps the larger set had broken down, he asked why the small one was there. 'Oh,' his brother-in-law replied, 'we have decided to watch less TV.'

❖

Approaching a passerby, a beggar asked, 'Sir, would you give me a hundred rupees for a cup of coffee?'

'That's ridiculous!' the man replied.

'Just a yes or no, fellow,' the beggar

growled. 'I don't need a lecture about how to run my business.'

❖

A man saw an epitaph in a cemetery that read: 'Here lies an honest man and politician.'

'Shame,' he said, 'two people in the same grave.'

❖

A jungle-witch-doctor was called to treat a man with high fever. He made a medicine with the eye of a toad, the liver of a snake, the heart of a rat, six black beetles and half a cockroach, all mixed together with slime from the local river.

The next day he went to see his patient and found him no better. 'Oh dear,' said the witch doctor. 'Maybe you had better y a couple of aspirins.'

❖

'Last week, a grain of sand got into my wife's eye, and she had to go to the doctor,' the married man told his friend. 'It cost me a hundred and fifty rupees.'

'That's nothing,' his friend replied. 'Last week a cocktail dress took my wife's eye, and it cost me fifteen hundred rupees.'

❖

The judge addresses the man in the courtroom: 'Don't you feel ashamed, coming here for the third time?'

The man replies: 'I'm here for the third time, but you come here every day!'

❖

An attorney was on his deathbed in the hospital. When a friend came to visit, he found the lawyer frantically going through the Gita.

'What are you doing?' the visitor asked.

The sick lawyer replied, 'Looking for loopholes.'

❖

The psychiatrist asks his patient: 'Do you ever hear voices without knowing who is speaking or where they are coming from?'

'Yes, of course I do.'

'And when does this happen?'

'When I answer the phone!'

❖

'Stop, Look, Listen!'

Wonderful words. These three words illustrate the whole scheme of married life. You see a pretty girl. You stop; you look. After that you marry her and then for the rest of your life, you listen!

❖

The signboard on the door of a lawyer's chamber reads: 'Where there is a will, there is a way; where there is a way, there is law; where there is law, there is a rule; where there is a rule, there is a loophole; where there is a loophole, there is a lawyer; and here I am, your advocate.'

❖

After having examined the lady thoroughly, the doctor explained his prescription as he wrote it out. 'Take the green pill with a glass of water when you get up. Take the blue pill with a glass of water after lunch. Then just before going to bed, take the red pill with another glass of water.'

'Exactly what is my problem, Doctor?' the woman asked.

'You're not drinking enough water.'

❖

Walking down the street, a dog saw a sign in an office window. 'Help wanted. Must type seventy words a minute. Must be computer literate. Must be bilingual. An equal-opportunity employer.'

The dog applied for the position, but he was quickly rebuffed. 'I can't hire a dog for this job,' the office manager said. But when the dog pointed to the line that read 'An equal-opportunity employer', the office manager sighed and asked, 'Can you type?' Silently, the dog walked over to a typewriter and flawlessly banged out a letter. 'Can you operate a computer?' the manager enquired. The dog then sat down at a terminal, wrote a programme and ran it perfectly.

'Look, I still can't hire a dog for this position,' said the exasperated office manager. 'You have fine skills, but I need someone who's bilingual. It says so right in the ad.'

The dog looked up at the manager and said, 'Meow.'

When his grandparents celebrated their fiftieth wedding anniversary, Grandpa asked Grandma, 'Have you been loyal to me all these years?' After some gentle persuasion she told him that, for every disloyal thought she had ever had, she had placed one pea in a glass container in the kitchen. Grandpa rushed off, and on his return expressed relief in finding only three peas. 'Well,' she replied with a grin, 'I have made pea soup a couple of times.'

❖

When Paul was working as a salesman at a supermarket, he noticed that before choosing a melon, shoppers would hold the fruit upto their ears and knock on it. He never knew what they expected to hear. One day he asked a shopper about it. 'Son,' the shopper replied, 'I've been doing this for forty years. All I know is that if you just pick it up and put it in your bag, everybody looks at you as if you're crazy.'

While revisiting the town where she had worked as a nurse years before, an elderly woman met a middle-aged farmer, 'Bert,' she said, 'I can remember back to the time when I used to put diapers on you.'

Bert was stone deaf, but realized that the woman wanted to be friendly. So he nodded and said, 'Yes indeed, ma'am, things have changed. You'd hardly recognize the old place now.'

❖

During a summer holiday, a man took a part-time job as a plumber. A few days later he was required to repair a leaking tap, and assured the caller that he would be there in a few minutes. Unfortunately, the van was being repaired, and he was delayed at least two hours. It took another hour to get through the rush-hour traffic, and when he finally arrived, the door was opened by an irate woman. Putting on his brightest smile, he asked, 'Are you the woman with the leaking tap?'

'I was,' she replied. 'Now I'm the woman with the indoor pool.'

❖

A hammer sometimes misses its mark, a bouquet never.

❖

A Scotsman, applying for admission to the police force, was being given a test in general knowledge. 'Now then,' said the inspector, glowering, 'how would you act in dispersing a large and argumentative crowd?'

'Well,' replied the Scotsman, 'I'm not too sure how ye do it here. But in Aberdeen we just pass the hat around, and they soon begin to shuffle off.'

❖

Lord Thomson, the tight-fisted Canadian newspaper baron and owner of the *Times*, was driving to the office with his son, Ken, joint chairman of a worldwide conglomerate now estimated to be worth many millions.

'What's that?' Thomson demanded as Ken unfolded his morning paper.

'The *Times*.'

'And where did you get it?' enquired Thomson.

'At the shop round the corner.'

'Well, Ken,' his lordship said anxiously, 'you take it right back and let someone else buy it. You can have mine when I have finished.'

❖

A busy country doctor often covered the thirty kilometres to the nearest hospital with more regard for expediency than the speed limit. One day, he took his five-year-old son along for the ride when he went to make hospital rounds. Afterwards, his wife asked their son if he had enjoyed it. 'It was neat,' replied the son. 'A nice man on a motorcycle stopped us and wrote father a prescription.'

❖

The husband was the army's chief engineer in Bombay when the city was very short of water. The army nurses' mess was particularly hard hit and, after the nurses jointly appealed to him, he arranged for them to get a larger quota.

A few days later, the chief engineer and his wife were invited for a party at the nurses' mess. As they were being introduced to everybody, an attractive young probationer turned to the husband and gushed: 'Oh sir, whenever I take off my clothes for a bath I think of you!'

❖

Sign in a New York store: 'Complaints department on the forty-fifth floor. Lift out of order; please use the stairs.'

❖

A boy asked his father, 'Dad, how much does it cost to get married?'

'I don't know,' replied his father, 'I am still paying.'

❖

A woman took her radio to a repair shop, explained that there seemed to be something loose inside it, and hurried out to catch a bus.

Two weeks later, she went to the shop to see if the work had been done. She had not given them her name, so she described the radio and what had been wrong with it. The assistant found the radio. It had a ticket reading, 'Lady, screw loose.'

❖

Minister to aides, discussing Seventh Five Year Plan: 'Why again food, employment, etc.? We gave them all that in the first plan itself, didn't we?'

❖

Charlie had trouble hearing till he went to the neighbourhood doctor, who promptly extracted a dime from the guy's ear.

'You're marvellous!' cried Charlie. 'I can hear perfectly now. It was there for three months!'

'You mean you knew it? Why didn't you take it out?' asked the baffled doctor.

Charlie shrugged his shoulders: 'I didn't need the money.'

❖

A girl and boy squirrel were chattering and playing around when up comes a fox. The girl squirrel quickly ran up a tree.

The boy squirrel stayed on the ground.

'That's odd,' said the fox, 'squirrels are afraid of me and run up a tree as a rule.'

'Listen, bud,' said the boy squirrel, 'did you ever try to climb a tree when you were in love?'

❖

A woman drove up to her home, staggered out of her car and into the arms of her husband, gasping: 'Wow! It is so hot! I thought I'd pass out.'

'But why didn't you open the windows of the car while you were driving?'

'Oh no!' she answered, 'I want the neighbours to think we have an air-conditioned car.'

❖

An elderly lady was sitting in her rocking chair knitting, her Persian cat reclining at her feet. Suddenly a fairy appeared and asked the old lady if there was anything she wished for. 'Yes,' was the reply, 'I would like to be a young woman again.' The fairy waved her wand and there she stood, a lovely girl of eighteen!

'Now,' asked the fairy, 'is there any other wish you would like granted?'

'Oh yes, I would like a handsome young man.'

Turning to the cat, the fairy waved her wand, and in its place rose a fine looking youth. He looked sadly at the girl and sighed, 'Now aren't you sorry you took me to the vet?'

❖

It was their twenty-fifth wedding anniversary, and he promised her anything she wanted.

'Do you remember when you proposed to me?' she said. 'You got down on your knees and said, "I love you." That's what I'd like you to do again.'

'Are you kidding?' he frowned.

'No. I'm serious.'

'Okay,' he said as he got down on both knees. 'Dear, I love you; now help me up!'

❖

The excited couple had the county clerk hurriedly fill in the marriage licence, and they then dashed over to the Justice of the Peace.

'I'm sorry,' said the Justice, when he looked at the licence, 'but it doesn't have the girl's name on it.'

'Can't you put it in?' asked the girl.

'No indeed,' said the Justice, 'You'll have to take it back to the county clerk.'

So they hurried back to the clerk and when they returned to the Justice, he looked at the licence again and said, 'There's no date on it.'

'But can't you . . .'

'Nope.'

So back to the clerk they went. Once

more they appeared before the Justice and this time he said, 'It doesn't have the county seal on it. And don't ask me to put the seal on. That's not my job. Take it back to the clerk.'

Thoroughly disgusted, the couple went back to the county clerk; and at last returned to the Justice. 'Well, that's better,' said the Justice as he approved the licence. He then noticed the three-year-old boy with the couple.

'Whose boy is that?' he asked.

'Ours,' answered the girl.

'Yours? That means you had the child before you . . .'

'Yes, before we were married.'

'Well, I suppose that's not my affair,' said the Justice, 'but I hope you realize that this boy is a technical bastard.'

'Isn't that strange,' retorted the young father, 'That's exactly what the county clerk said you were!'

❖

Three heads of state went to meet God. Asked the American head-of-state, 'Dear God, when will corruption end in my country?'

Said God, 'In another fifty years.' The premier broke down and started crying.

'Oh! God,' the American sobbed, 'I am so depressed that corruption will not be wiped out during my lifetime.'

Then came the elderly Japanese head-of-state. Asked he, 'Dear God, when will corruption end in my country?'

And God said, 'In another thirty years.' He too broke down and sobbed, 'Oh! God! I am so depressed that corruption will not be wiped out during my lifetime.'

Then came the Indian head-of-state's chance to ask: 'Dear God, when will corruption end in my country?' At this, God broke down and wept copiously. 'I am so depressed,' God lamented, 'corruption will not be wiped out in your country during my lifetime.'

❖

Two strangers struck up a pleasant conversation as they sat in a bar. Time passed and several hours later the bartender announced last drinks. 'Say,' one of the drinkers asked his newfound friend, 'what does your wife say when you stay out so late?'

'I'm not married,' replied the other.

'Not married! Then why do you stay out this late!'

❖

Time spent in laughing is time spent with the gods.

❖

The tank of live lobsters at the seafood restaurant where Peter works is always popular with younger patrons. Once, he was showing the lobsters to an angelic-looking six-year-old girl, who petted one of them and said, 'Gee, I wish I could take it home with me.'

'Why?' Peter asked. 'Do you want to eat it?'

'No,' she replied. 'I want to feed my little brother to it.'

❖

While closing up a health club one night, the caretaker went to check the women's locker room to make sure it had been properly cleaned. He was about to knock on the door when he heard a woman inside yelling, 'Liar! Liar! Why can't you cooperate once in a while!'

As she rushed angrily past him, he asked her how many other members were still getting changed. 'None,' she fumed. He walked in, wondering who had angered her. Then he spotted the upright scale. The weight bar was still shaking from her hasty departure.

❖

Once there was a boy whose parents named him Odd. Other children used to tease him about his name, but he stuck out his chest and refused to be bothered. As he grew up, people continued to make fun of this, even after he became a successful attorney. Finally, as an old man, he wrote out his last wishes. 'I've been the butt of jokes all my life,' he said. 'I'll not have people making fun of me after I'm gone.' He instructed that his tombstone should not bear his name.

After his death, people noticed the large blank stone and said, 'That's odd.'

❖

When a new manager took over the department, he called a meeting of all the staff. 'What I want,' he said, 'is extra effort from everyone. So let's get it together and see if we can increase productivity.'

A few days later, the Superintendent received two memos from members of staff requesting maternity leave and passed them on to the boss.

❖

'**D**o you think you could sunbathe topless in your garden for a change?' a woman asked the young woman next door.

'Why?' asked the neighbour, somewhat puzzled.

'Because it's time my husband mowed the lawn again!'

❖

The pastor in a certain village heard that a young man was behaving scandalously, so he went to speak to him. 'I've been told that you are raising false hopes in the hearts of many young girls,' the pastor said. 'You've promised marriage to one girl here, another in the next village and God knows how many more. How can you do something like that?'

'Well, pastor,' replied the suitor, 'I have a bicycle!'

❖

Sales manager to an applicant: 'Have you any previous sales experience?'

'Yes, sir, I sold my house, my car, the piano and almost all my wife's jewellery.'

❖

Jesus, Moses and God were out playing golf. Jesus teed off first and the ball flew straight over the fairway, landed on the green and rolled to within a couple of feet off the hole. Moses hit second, and his ball also soared and landed close to the hole. Both looked over at God. God took a few practice swings, then let loose on his ball. The ball flew off into the rough. Just then a squirrel jumped over, grabbed the ball in its mouth and started running across the fairway. An eagle scooped down and grabbed the squirrel in its claws, but before it could get too far, a bolt of lightning struck the bird. The ball fell and a sudden gust of wind blew it and dropped it directly into the hole.

Jesus glared at God and said: 'Hey, are you here to play golf or just fool around!'

❖

The brand new married couple entrained for their honeymoon to Florida. Before long, a train conductor came through collecting tickets. The groom absent-mindedly handed over the marriage license. The conductor examined the paper and said, 'Young man, this may be good for a lot of rides but not on this train.'

❖

Lawyer Nathaniel liked to tell the story of a young lady who tried to engage his services for a seduction suit against her employer. Nathaniel told her she had insufficient facts to support such an action. She was very downcast when she left him, but returned triumphant the following morning, to report, 'He seduced me again last night.'

❖

A girl had just received an engagement ring and excitedly wore it into the office the next day. To her exasperation, no one noticed it. After squirming through half the morning, she exclaimed loudly: 'My goodness, it's hot in here. I think I'll take this ring off?'

❖

The authorities were investigating the mysterious death of a prosperous businessman who had jumped from a window of his office. His sexy private secretary could offer no explanation for the action, but said that her employer had been acting strangely ever since she started working for him a month ago. 'After my very first week in the office,' she said, 'I received a twenty-five-dollar raise. After the second week, he called me into his private office, gave me a lovely black negligee, five pairs of nylon stockings, and said, 'These are for a beautiful, capable secretary.' At the end of the third week, he gave me a precious mink stole. Then, on that afternoon he called me into his private office again, presented me with this fabulous diamond bracelet, and asked me if I would consider making love to him and what it would cost. 'I told him I would and since he had been so nice to me, it would only cost him five dollars, although I was charging all the other boys in the office ten. That's when he jumped out of the window.'

❖

Ben doesn't worry about talking in the sleep. His wife and mistress have the same name.

❖

The drunk lurched to the elevator, opened the door, and stepped in. Unfortunately, the elevator was not there, and he plopped the six stories to the bottom of the shaft. Dusting himself off, he scowled and shouted, 'Dammit, I said "up".'

❖

'**I** have seven children and I've just found out my husband has never really loved me,' said the distraught woman to her lawyer.

'There, there, my dear,' said the attorney, 'Just imagine the fix you'd be in today if he had.'

❖

An executive friend of ours is so dedicated to his work that he keeps his secretary near his bed in case he gets an idea during the night.

❖

Myrtle is the treasurer of her social club and has had no difficulty in the safekeeping of the funds. Therefore, when her bank called her to advise that her balance was overdrawn, she was quite disturbed.

'How much am I overdrawn?' she asked. The bank manager told her: 'Twenty dollars.'

'Look here,' said Myrtle. 'What was my balance last month?'

'Three hundred dollars,' replied the manager.

'Well?' asked Myrtle. 'Did I call you up?'

❖

As a new, rather shy physical therapist, Cathy enjoyed conversing with her patients but would become uncomfortable when questioned about her personal life. One day a hundred-year-old woman, after learning she was married, asked if they had any children. When Cathy told her no, she countered, 'And why not?' 'We're both just starting careers,' Cathy replied, 'and we don't have the time.' This silenced her for a moment while Cathy sighed with relief. Then she shook her head, patted her on the hand and said, 'Sweetie, it only takes fifteen minutes.'

❖

'The thrill is gone from my marriage,' Alan told his friend Don.

'Why not add some intrigue to your life . . . like have an affair?' Don suggested.

'But what if my wife finds out?'

'Heck, this is the twenty-first century, Alan. Go ahead and tell her about it!'

So Alan went home and said, 'Dear, I think an affair will bring us closer together.'

'Forget it,' his wife replied unperturbed, 'I've tried that but it never worked.'

❖

On a cold night, a man with reputedly poor eyesight was driving a friend home. The frost was thick on the windows, and after a couple of near accidents the friend tactfully suggested that it might help if they cleaned the windscreen. 'What's the use?' the driver replied. 'I left my glasses at home.'

❖

An indignant traveller wrote to the railways: 'I take your 9.35 a.m. train daily. I cannot get a seat near the front of the train and sometimes have to stand all the way.

Several coaches on this train near the back carry very few passengers. Will you please advise me why those coaches cannot be put on the front of the train so that we won't be so crowded?'

❖

'She told me,' a woman complained to a friend, 'that you told her the secret I told you not to tell her.'

'Well,' replied her friend in a hurt tone, 'I told her not to tell you that I told her.'

'Oh, dear,' sighed the first woman. 'Well, don't tell her I told you that she told me.'

❖

In answer to a quiz question, 'What is the first thing you notice about a girl?' A young man said, 'It depends on which way she's going.'

Statistics are like a bikini bathing suit. What they reveal is suggestive, but what they conceal is vital.

❖

My five-year-old son went with me to see a young couple's new baby. He gazed at the small red, wrinkled face a long time, then murmured solemnly, 'So that's why she hid him under her coat for so long.'

❖

The US theatrical manager cabled an European actress asking what salary she wanted to appear in a play in New York. She demanded a thousand dollars a week.

'Accepted thousand with pleasure,' the manager wired back.

'Thousand for acting,' she promptly wired back. 'Pleasure extra.'

❖

My wife asked me to post a letter at the railway station. 'Please don't forget,' she said. 'It's important.' But I did forget, and was walking out of the station when a man tapped me on the shoulder. 'Remember the letter,' he said.

As I made my way to the nearest mailbox, another man called after me: 'Don't forget the letter.' But how on earth could these strangers know I was supposed to post a letter? When a third person reminded me, I blurted out: 'How do you know about it? And to set your mind at rest, I've just posted it.'

'In that case,' the stranger said, smiling, 'we may safely remove the label pinned to your back.'

The label read: 'Remind him to post that letter!'

❖

Police officer: You are drunk and yet you are driving very fast. Why?

Driver: I want to reach home before I cause an accident.

❖

Bachelors know more about women than married men do; that's why they are bachelors.

❖

Teacher: Manish, what is meant by an autobiography?
Manish: The life-story of cars, sir.

❖

Teacher: 'I sleep'. Change this sentence into future tense.
Student: I wake up.

❖

Three men were standing in line to get

into heaven one day. Apparently it had been a pretty busy day, so St. Peter had to tell the first one, 'Heaven's getting pretty close to full today, and I've been asked to admit only people who have had particularly horrible deaths. So what's your story?'

So the first man replies: 'Well, for a while I've suspected my wife and once I came home early to catch her red-handed but found no one hiding in my twenty-fifth floor apartment. When I went out to the balcony, I saw this man hanging off the railing, twenty-five floors above ground!

'It drove me really mad, so I started beating on him and kicking him, but he wouldn't fall off. I started hammering on his fingers. Of course, he couldn't stand that for long, so he let go and fell, but even after hurtling down twenty-five stories, he fell into the bushes, stunned but okay.

'I couldn't stand it anymore, so I ran into the kitchen, grabbed the fridge and threw it over the edge where it landed on him, killing him instantly. But all the stress and anger got to me, and I had a heart attack and died there on the balcony.'

'That sounds like a pretty bad day to me,' said St. Peter, and let the man in.

The second man comes up and when asked for his story he explains. 'It's been a very strange day. You see, I live on the twenty-sixth floor of my apartment building, and every morning I do my exercises out on my balcony. Well, this morning I must have slipped or something, because I fell over the edge. But I got lucky, and caught the railing of the balcony on the floor below me.

'I knew it couldn't hang on for very long, when suddenly this man burst out onto the balcony. I thought for sure I was saved, when he started beating on me and kicking me. I held on the best I could until he ran into the apartment and grabbed a hammer and started pounding on my hands.

'Finally I just let go, but again I got lucky and fell into the bushes below, stunned but all right. Just when I was thinking I was going to be okay, this refrigerator comes falling out of the sky and crushes me instantly, and now I'm here.'

Once again St. Peter had to concede that that sounded like a pretty horrible death.

The third man came to the front of the line and when asked for his story began, 'Picture this,' says the third man, 'I'm hiding naked inside a refrigerator . . .'

❖

'Gentlemen of the jury,' said the defence attorney, now beginning to warm to his summation, 'the real question here before you is, shall this beautiful young woman be forced to languish away her loveliest years in a dark prison cell? Or, shall she be set free to return to her cozy little apartment at 4134 Seaside Street, to spend her lonely, loveless hours in her boudoir, lying beside her little phone, 962-7873?'

❖

Moving along a dimly lit street, a person was suddenly approached by a stranger who had slipped from the shadows nearby.

'Please, sir,' asked the stranger, 'Would you be so kind as to help a poor unfortunate fellow who is hungry and out of work? All I have in the world is this gun.'

❖

Have you heard about the newlywed who was so lazy that he took his wife to the bridal suit of a hotel and waited for an earthquake?

❖

Economists are still trying to figure out why the girl with the least principle draws the most interest.

❖

A father received a birthday parcel from his son who was away at school. Inside was a set of inexpensive cuff links and a matching tie pin with this note: 'Dear Father: This isn't much, but it's all you can afford.'

❖

When a rumour got round that a certain farmer was underpaying his labour, an official came to check up.

'How many people do you employ?' he inquired.

'Two men,' said the farmer.

'I understand that you are paying them below the minimum wage,' the official said.

'Is that so,' snorted the farmer. He called the men.

'Now,' he said, 'tell this fellow what your wages are.'

'Forty dollars a week,' each of them answered.

'Well, that's all right,' the official said. He turned to the farmer, 'Are you sure you don't employ anyone else?'

'Only a half-wit,' the farmer said. 'He gets his board and a little cash each week for his tobacco.'

'That's disgraceful,' the official said. 'Let me talk to him!'

'Talk to him!' the farmer said. 'You're talking to him now.'

❖

At the farm auction the bidding was particularly brisk for an old hand-blown whisky bottle, and finally a collector was the successful bidder at twenty dollars. When his purchase was handed over to him, an aged but sharp-eyed farmer nearby leant over and took a good look at the bottle.

'My God,' he gasped to a friend, 'it's empty!'

❖

We know an insurance salesman who says his greatest successes are with young housewives who aren't adequately covered.

❖

A man telephoned a police station one night, and excitedly reported that the steering wheel, brake pedal, accelerator, clutch pedal and dashboard had been stolen from his car. A sergeant promised to investigate. But soon the telephone rang again.

'Don't bother,' said the same voice, this time with a hiccup. 'I got into the back seat by mistake.'

When a man was taken to hospital after a car crash, the doctor, after examining him and putting his leg in a cast, said that he could go home the next day. In the morning, however, he announced: 'I think you'd better stay another day to see if something new turns up. I didn't know how badly you were smashed up until I read about the accident in the newspaper today.'

❖

A foreigner about to leave India was asked by his highly unsatisfactory manservant for a letter of recommendation. He pondered a moment, then wrote: 'To Whom It May Concern. The bearer of this note, Raju Ram, has served me during the last two years to his complete satisfaction. If you are thinking of giving him a berth, be sure to make it a wide one.'

❖

A Scotsman had just won a new car in a raffle but, far from being elated, he seemed decidedly glum. 'What's the matter, Jock?' asked a friend.

'Mon,' he answered, 'it's this other ticket. Why I ever bought it, I can't imagine.'

❖

The following conversation took place between a visiting American and an Eton schoolmaster. 'Do you allow your boys to smoke?' the American asked.

'I'm afraid not,' was the reply.

'Can they drink?'

'Good gracious, no.'

'What about dates?'

'Oh, that's quite all right,' said the master, 'as long as they don't eat too many.'

❖

A teacher of a girls' school smiled pleasantly at the gentleman sitting opposite her in the bus. He did not respond. Realizing her error, she said aloud, 'Oh, please excuse me. I mistook you for the father of two of my children.' She got out at the next corner.

❖

As doctors hovered anxiously nearby, a three-year-old patient at a children's hospital left his wheelchair on direction and began to walk clutching both hands tightly against his waist.

'Can't you move your hands, son?' asked the solicitous doctors.

'No,' said the boy.

The doctors asked again, 'Do your hands hurt?'

'No.'

'Will you try and move them for me?' asked one kindly doctor.

'No,' replied the boy. 'I've got to hold

up my pyjama trousers.

❖

British actress Joyce Grenfell recalls that while she and her friend Viola Tunnard were on hospital tour in India during the Second World War, they were invited to a service club dance at Poona. 'We were made to feel irresistible; lines formed to await our favours on the dance floor,' she writes. 'But we were a little surprised to hear ourselves announced as "two well-known artists who have been flown out from home to entertain men in bed."'

❖

Wife reading husband's fortune card from scale: 'You are a leader, with a magnetic personality and strong character. You are intelligent, witty and attractive to the opposite sex.' She paused, 'It has your weight wrong too.'

❖

The transferred clergyman was being praised by members of his congregation. One woman told him: 'You're wonderful! I never knew what sin was till you came here.'

❖

A London doctor prescribed for Robinson, who was overweight, a drastic pill to be taken before retiring on six successive nights. The first night after taking the pill, Robinson dreamt that he was shipwrecked on a South Sea island with a beautiful maiden. He chased her all over the island and woke up in a sweat when he couldn't catch her. The marathon continued for six nights until he had lost ten kilos.

A friend, Brown, who was also rather portly, commented on his slim, healthy look, heard the story and said, 'I'll have to see that doctor myself.' But after taking his first pill, Brown had a different dream. He landed on the island, all right, but there was no beautiful maiden for him. Instead, a highly decorated mob of savages pursued him ruthlessly for six nights. He, too, lost ten kilos.

Brown decided to go back to the doctor to enquire why his friend Robinson had lost as much weight, but apparently had a far more enjoyable time in his dreams.

'Mr Robinson, is a private patient,' said the doctor loftily. 'You, Mr Brown, are a Government Health Scheme patient.'

❖

If a window of opportunity appears, don't pull down the shade.

❖

A visiting clergyman was warned that

some of the congregation usually left before the end of the sermon. When he rose to begin his sermon, he announced, 'I am going to speak to two classes of people this morning; first to the sinners, then to the saints.' He proceeded to address the 'sinners' for a while, and then said they could leave. For once, every member of the congregation stayed to the end of the sermon.

❖

A teacher was giving her pupils a lesson in logic. 'Here is the situation,' she said. 'A man is standing up in a boat in the middle of a river, fishing. He loses his balance, falls in, and begins splashing and yelling for help. His wife hears the commotion, knows he can't swim, and runs down to the bank. Why do you think she ran to the bank?'

A girl raised her hand and asked, 'To draw out all his savings?'

Let me tell you about two frogs who jumped into a bucket of cream on a dairy farm.

'May as well give up,' croaked one after trying in vain to get out. 'We're going to die.'

'Keep on paddling,' said the other frog. 'We'll get out of this mess somehow.'

'It's no use,' said the first. 'Too thick to swim. Too thin to jump. Too slippery to crawl. We are bound to die some time any way. So it may as well be tonight.' He sank to the bottom of the bucket and died.

His friend just kept on paddling, and paddling and paddling. And by morning he was perched on a mass of butter which he had churned all by himself. There he was, with a grin on his face, eating the flies that came swamping from every direction.

That little frog had discovered what most people ignore: if you stick with the task long enough, you're going to be a winner.

A khaddar-clad minister visits the Maruti car factory. The manager goes out of the way to show him around and at the end of the tour, offers the minister a free car.

'Oh, no,' says the minister, 'I cannot accept it.'

'In that case I'll sell it to you for five hundred rupees.' The minister hands the manager two five-hundred rupee notes. 'In that case, I'll have two.'

❖

Two computer analysts were riding a bike one day when one analyst asked the other, 'Hey Sam, where did you get such a great bike?'

The second analyst replied, 'Well, I was walking along yesterday, when a beautiful woman rode up on a bike and asked me to follow her. She led me deep into the forest and then flung the bike to the ground, took off her clothes and said,

"Take what you want." So I took the bike.'

The second analyst nodded approvingly, 'Good choice, Sam; after all, what would you have done with the clothes?'

❖

Reflect upon your present blessings . . . of which every man has many; not on your past misfortunes, of which all men have some.

❖

The devil challenged St.Peter to a game. 'How can you win?' St.Peter asked. 'All the famous players are up here.'

'How can I lose?' retorted Satan. 'All the umpires are down here.'

❖

A young man who had just passed the

bar exam, was being interviewed by a prestigious law firm. 'What would you do,' a partner enquired, 'if a prospective client asked for counsel on a subject you knew nothing about?'

'I would tell the client,' the applicant replied without hesitation, 'to give me a retainer of five thousand rupees and call me in the morning.'

❖

'**M**y husband and I never argue,' said one woman to another.

'Not even when he's right?'

'I don't know. That's never happened.'

❖

Little Johnny was practising the violin in the living room, while his father was trying to read in living room. The family dog was lying in the den and as the screeching sounds of little Johnny's violin reached his ears, he began to howl loudly. The father listened to the dog and the violin for as long as he could. Then he jumped up, slammed his newspaper on the floor and yelled above the noise, 'For God's sake, can't you play something the dog doesn't know?'

❖

Once there was a fellow who was too forward. He would meet a girl and within two seconds say, 'Honey, let's make love.' His buddy took him aside and explained that he should act suave and carry on a friendly conversation for a while, before he suggested such things.

On his next date the young man remembered the words of wisdom. He started the conversation by saying, 'Honey, have you ever been to Africa?'

She said, 'No.'

So he said, 'Well, let's make love.'

❖

The customer had just returned to a restaurant for the first time after a long while and the girls had all been outfitted in new uniforms. Across the left breast pocket on each uniform, the girl's names were embroidered. One of the waitresses faced him and said, 'How do you like it?'

'I like it very much,' he replied, 'but tell me, what are you going to name the other one?'

❖

The meek little man approached a policeman on the street corner.

'Excuse me, officer,' he said, 'but I've been waiting here for my wife for over an hour. Would you be kind enough to order me to move?'

❖

Woman: Your Honour, I want a divorce. My husband's been cheating on me.

Judge: That's a serious accusation Madam. Have you any evidence to substantiate your accusation?

Woman: Of course. While walking on Broadway the other night I saw him going into a movie theatre with another woman.

❖

You never really understand a person until you consider things from his or her point of view.

❖

'I'm sorry,' said the judge. 'Your daughter's only fifteen, Mrs Cove. I just can't issue a marriage licence to her.'

'Judge,' said Mrs Cove unhappily, 'are you telling me my daughter's too young to do what she's already gone and done?'

❖

The doctor gave his diagnosis to the flashy female who stood before him. 'This examination reveals a serious situation. I want you to refrain from relationships with your husband for several weeks. May I count on such cooperation?'

'Sure, Doc, that's no problem. I got a boyfriend you know.'

❖

It was Meera's first airplane trip and she was determined to be nonchalant about the whole thing. After reading a magazine for a while she yawned and glanced out of the window.

'My,' she said, 'people really look just like ants from this height.'

'Lady,' said a fellow passenger. 'We haven't taken off yet. Those *are* ants.'

❖

As Peter entered the police station the

other evening to pay a parking fine, he noticed that an old lady just ahead of him was trembling all over. He paid his money and was about to leave when he saw the lady sitting on a bench in the corner absorbed in a book. 'What's the trouble,' he asked. 'Is there anything I can do?'

'No, thank you,' she replied sedately. 'You see, I was sitting at home all alone reading this murder story, and I got so scared that I came down here to finish it under police protection.'

❖

In its campaign to recruit paratroopers, badly needed in North Africa, the French Army achieved notable success with a poster at one of the busiest thoroughfares of Paris, reading: 'Young men! Join the parachutist forces of France. It is more dangerous to cross this street than to jump with a parachute.'

But the spell of the advertisement was

broken when someone scribbled at the bottom: 'I would gladly join, but the recruiting office is on the other side of the street!'

❖

Trying to eclipse his brother's gift of a Cadillac, a Hollywood producer paid ten thousand dollars for an amazing mynah bird to present it to his mother on her birthday. The bird spoke eleven languages and sang grand opera.

On the night of her birthday he put through a long-distance call. 'What did you think of the bird, Mamma?' he asked.

'Delicious!' she said.

❖

While attending a convention, Carol and John were taken out to dinner by another couple. Carol, who could never remember names, had to ask her husband the hosts' names twice during the meal and again on return to the hotel. In exasperation, John chided her about her lack of attention and ended the lecture saying that he was surprised she could remember his name even after twenty years of marriage.

'Well,' she said, 'why do you think I call you "honey" most of the time?'

❖

She: My mother says that there are some things that a girl should not do before twenty.
He: Well, personally, I don't like a large audience either.

❖

Swiftly he climbed the ladder and tapped on his beloved's window-pane for eloping. 'Are you all packed?' he called.

'Hush,' said the girl. 'Father may

hear you. I think I hear him in the next room.'

'Can't be,' said the youth. 'He's holding the ladder.'

❖

The shy young girl from the country was on her first city date and was thrilled beyond words. She didn't want to appear countrified: she had put on her prettiest dress, got a sophisticated hairdo, and was all prepared to talk understandingly about art, music or politics.

Her escort took her to a movie, and then to his favourite cafe. 'Two beers,' he told the waiter.

She, not to be outdone, murmured, 'The same for me.'

❖

A naive young man who had lived a sheltered life, finally decided he couldn't take any more. He arranged an appointment with his doctor and poured out the whole story.

'It's this girl I've been going with,' he said. 'I suspected she was fast, but I never dreamt she was a sex maniac. Every night, now for weeks and weeks on end, I keep trying to break off the romance, but I haven't got the will power. What can I do? My health just can't stand the pace.'

'I see,' said the doctor grimly. 'Tell me just what happens; you can trust me.'

❖

An experienced plumber was giving instructions to his apprentice.

'Working in other people's homes,' he said, 'can sometimes lead to embarrassing situations, but you can always get out of them by using tact. For example, the other day, I walked into a bathroom and found a lady taking a bath. I backed out saying, "Excuse me, sir." In that way, the lady thought I hadn't gotten a good look at her and it was all right.'

The following afternoon, the apprentice staggered into the office in a beaten-up condition.

'What happened to you?' asked the boss.

'You and your tact,' cried the apprentice. 'I went to the bridal suite of the Etter Plaza Hotel to fix a faucet. I was half-way through the bedroom before I realized there was a couple making love in the bed. The husband cussed at me, but I remembered what you had said, so I tipped my hat and said, "Excuse me, gentlemen!"'

❖

The two playboys were comparing notes.

'I saw you out on the town last night.' said one. 'How'd you make out?'

'The greatest!' replied his friend. 'I met this lady taxi driver, and what a terrific time we had!'

'A lady taxi driver?' puzzled the first. 'How could you tell?'

'Easy,' answered the other, 'I knew she was a taxi driver because all night long she kept going out on calls.'

❖

One afternoon two women met on the golf course. In addition to belonging to the same country club, they had one thing more in common; one had recently married the ex-husband of the other.

The original wife spoke up, 'Although we didn't get along, I must admit he was an ardent lover. When it came to making love, he was dynamite.'

'Well,' complained the present wife, 'he may have been dynamite to you, but he must have blown his fuse!'

❖

The silver lining is easier to find in someone else's cloud.

❖

One of the two drunks standing beside a lamp post, asked his companion, 'Shay, you gotta match?'

'I think sho,' said his companion. 'Lemme shee.' He reached in his pocket, withdrew a match stick and rubbed the unsulphured end on the lamp post several times. 'No good,' he said finally, and threw it away. He pulled out another and tried again to strike the unsulphured end. 'No good,' he said again, and threw it away. He reached into his pocket, found another match, and fortunately tried to light the proper end. It blazed up, but immediately he blew it out and thrust it back into his pocket. 'Ah,' he beamed. 'Thash a good one. Gotta save it.'

❖

Hoping to avoid the embarrassing attention that most hotels bestow on newlyweds, the honeymooners carefully removed the rice from their hair, took the JUST MARRIED sign off their car and even scruffed their luggage up to give it that travelled look. Then, without betraying a trace of their eagerness, they ambled casually into Miami Beach's Fontainebleu Hotel and up to the front desk, where the groom said in a loud booming voice, 'We'd like a double bed with a room.'

❖

Obsessed with the idea of pleasing all manner of customers with girls of the very highest order, an enterprising madam set up a three-storey house of sport. She had ex-secretaries, selected for their efficiency, on the first floor; ex-models, selected for their beauty, on the second; and ex-schoolteachers, selected for their intelligence, on the third. As time went on, the madam noticed that almost all the play went to floor number three. She asked why, and the answer to the puzzle finally came from one of the steady customers.

'Well,' said the sporting gentleman, 'you know how those schoolteachers are—they make you do it over and over, until you get it right.'

❖

Drawn by the crowd, we stopped in at a bookstore recently that had a huge sign in the window reading: NEWLY TRANSLATED FROM THE ORIGINAL FRENCH: 27 MATING POSITIONS.

Inside, copies of the book, pre-wrapped, were selling like hot cakes. It was only by accident that we heard one harried clerk say to another, after ringing up his 423rd sale of the volume for the day, 'This is really the most extraordinary sale I've ever seen for a chess book.'

❖

The newly-arrived Asian diplomat was being given a thorough tour of Washington night life by his State Department escort. After watching a group of young couples in a twist cafe, the escort said, 'I don't imagine you've ever seen anything quite like this in your country. Do you know what they're doing?'

'Yes', said the diplomat. 'But why are they standing up?'

❖

A night worker had let his whiskers grow until his favourite baseball team won the pennant, much to the disgust of his young and pretty wife. On the day his team clinched the pennant, he laid off work, got himself a shave, went home early and slipped into bed. He took his wife's hand in the darkness and placed it upon his smoothly shaven face. She turned slightly while running her fingers over the now smooth chin and said, 'Make it snappy, kid. Old Whiskers will be home any minute now.'

❖

Glancing from her window one morning, Mrs Kulick was shocked to see her maid kissing the mikman. Highly incensed at such goings on, Mrs Kulick was determined to reprimand her servant.

Nadine was called into the parlour that night, before the family retired. Mrs Kulick frowned at the girl.

'Nadine,' she said sternly, 'this morning I saw you kissing the milkman. After this, I shall bring in the milk.'

'Tain't no use, Ma'am,' answered Nadine, 'he promised me he'd never kiss anyone but me.'

❖

A Russian lecturer was telling Czech students in Prague about the Soviet's wonderful scientific advances. 'Already,' he said, 'we have launched two satellites. In no time at all we will be able to go to the moon. In a matter of a few years we will be able to go to Mars, and then to Venus. And later on to all planets. Isn't this a wonderful thing?'

All the students nodded.

'Are there any questions?'

A student raised his hand. 'Sir,' he asked, 'when can we go to Vienna?'

❖

At a dinner party the hostess, whose kittenish ways were most annoying, produced a family album. 'This,' she said coyly, holding up a mother-and-child picture, 'is myself twenty-eight years ago.'

A guest examined the photograph, then asked slyly: 'Who is the baby in your lap?'

A woman drove into a service station to complain that her car was using up too much gas. The attendant pointed to the choke lever protruding from the dashboard. 'Do you know what this is for?' he asked.

'Oh, that,' said the woman airily. 'I never use it, so I keep it pulled out to hang my handbag on.'

❖

'This is the garage,' an excited voice proclaimed to a man over the phone. 'Your wife just drove your car in here to be repaired, and I want to know who's going to . . .'

'Okay, okay,' interrupted the man wearily. 'I'll pay for the car.'

'Who's worrying about that?' the voice continued. 'What I want to know is, who's going to pay to repair my garage?'

❖

A truck driver for an American firm had a collision. In filling in the required form, he stated that the accident was unavoidable. Under 'remarks', he wrote, 'The woman in front of me signaled a left turn and made a left turn.'

❖

To illustrate the importance of making prescriptions clear to patients, Dr William Osler used to tell his students this story:

A doctor once told a foreign patient, 'The thing for you to do is to drink hot water an hour before breakfast every morning.' After a week the man returned to the doctor's surgery. 'How are you feeling?' asked the physician.

'I feel worse if anything.'

'Did you follow my directions and drink hot water an hour before breakfast every morning?' asked the doctor.

'I tried my best,' replied the patient, 'but I couldn't keep it up for more than fifteen minutes at a time.'

❖

The doctor diagnosed the colonel's illness as hydropsy. What was that? Too much water in the body, the doctor explained. The whisky-drinking colonel was indignant. 'But I've never drunk a drop of water in all my life, doctor!' He paused. Then sadly, he concluded: 'Must have been the ice.'

❖

Desperate for work, a man went to the owner of a local circus and asked if there were any openings. The owner told him that he needed a high-wire act, but that the job required walking without a net over the lion's pit while wearing a monkey suit. In no position to quibble, the man took the job, put on the suit, and climbed to the high wire amid the stunned gasps of the crowd. Stepping gingerly on the thin cord, he began to shuffle his way across, but quickly lost his footing and tumbled into the lion's cage. 'Help!' the man screamed as the lion pounced on him. 'This beast is going to eat me!'

'Shut up,' the lion said angrily. 'You want to get us all fired?'

❖

A businessman taking a seminar on efficiency completed a case study of his wife's routine for fixing breakfast, and presented the results to the class. 'After a few days of observation, I quickly determined the practices that were robbing her of precious time and energy,' the man reported. 'Taking note of how many trips she made from the kitchen to the dining room carrying just one item, I suggested that in the future she carry several items at a time.'

'Did it work?' the teacher asked.

'It sure did,' replied the businessman. 'Instead of taking her twenty minutes to fix my breakfast, it now takes me just seven.'

❖

What an accident! He fell out of the upper berth and landed in the middle of a honeymoon.

❖

Four surgeons were taking a coffee break and comparing notes.

'I think accountants are the easiest to operate on,' the first one said. 'You open them up and everything is numbered.'

'I think librarians are the easiest to operate on,' the second one offered. 'You open them up and everything inside is in alphabetical order.'

The third one said, 'I like engineers— they always understand when you have parts left over at the end.'

'I prefer to operate on lawyers,' said the fourth surgeon, the most experienced of the group. 'They're heartless, spineless and gutless, and their heads and rear ends are interchangeable.'

❖

A young man was in court for stealing a boombox from an electronics store, but he told the judge that it wasn't his intention to keep the radio. 'I was just taking it for a joke, to see if anyone noticed it missing,' he remarked.

'Since you took it all the way home,' said the judge, 'I'm going to give you thirty days for carrying a joke too far.'

❖

Scientists have recently discovered a food that greatly reduces sex drive—it's called wedding cake.

In a bar a young bachelor told an older man that he was looking for a girl to marry. The latter smiled. 'Fortunately,' he said, 'I have a daughter of marriageable age. She has eyes like a doe, lips like rosebuds, ears like coral shells, a neck like a swan and a voice like a nightingale. She'd be ideal for you.'

'I'm not sure,' replied the bachelor. 'She doesn't seem human.'

❖

A seedy-looking man was sitting in the first row at a town meeting, heckling the mayor as he delivered a lengthy speech. Finally the mayor pointed to the heckler and said, 'Will that gentleman who differs with me please stand up and tell the audience what has he ever done for the good of the city?'

'Well, Mr Mayor,' the man said in a firm voice. 'I voted against you in the last election.'

At a senior citzens' function, I watched an older fellow tease his wife ahead of him in line.

'You ask for the tickets, dear,' he told her. 'You look older than I do.'

Seeming to ignore his uncomplimentary remark, she stepped up to the counter. 'I'd like two tickets, please,' she said loudly. 'One for me and one for my father.'

❖

The greatest pleasure I know is to do a good action by stealth, and have it found out by accident.

❖

Just before throwing a lavish party at his state, a tycoon had his swimming-pool filled with poisonous snakes. He called the guests together and announced, 'To anyone brave enough to swim across this pool, I will give the choice of a thousand hectares of my oil fields, ten thousand heads of cattle or my daughter's hand in marriage.'

No sooner were his words spoken than a young man plunged in, swam across the pool and climbed out unscathed but breathless.

'Congratulations!' the tycoon greeted him. "Do you want my oil fields?"

'No,' gasped the guest.

"The ten thousand heads of cattle?"

'No!' the young man shouted.

'Well, how about my daughter's . . .'

'No.'

'You must want something,' said the puzzled host.

'I just want to know the name of the guy who pushed me in!'

❖

Waiting in court to give evidence in a protracted case, I decided to go listen to a different case. As I entered, a barrister was finishing his apparently long and tedious argument for a defendant who, it was obvious, was likely to go to prison.

'If you are of a mind to give my client a prison sentence, Your Honour,' he closed, 'I hope you will think of it in terms of months rather than years.'

'Certainly,' the judge replied. 'Sixty months. Take him down.'

❖

Every time Paul tried to start the car, his driving instructor found something to criticize. But this time, every gesture would be carefully thought out, perfect. He adjusted the seat and mirrors, buckled up, coordinated the clutch, handbrake and gears, gave the accelerator a little push—and nothing happened. Silence.

The instructor coughed. 'What about starting the engine?' he suggested politely.

A wealthy matron is so proud of a valuable antique vase that she decides to have her bedroom painted the same colour as the vase. Several painters try to match the shade, but none comes close enough to satisfy the eccentric woman. Eventually, a painter approaches who is confident he can mix the proper colour. The woman is pleased with the result, and the painter becomes famous.

Years later, he retires and turns the business over to his son. 'Dad,' says the son, 'there is something I have got to know. How did you get those walls to match that vase so perfectly?'

'Son,' the father replies, 'I painted the vase.'

❖

Divorce lawyer: I have succeeded in making a settlement with your husband that's completely fair to both of you.
Client: Fair to both of us! I could have done

that myself. What do you think I hired a lawyer for?

❖

There's an Indian, a Pakistani and a beautiful girl sitting next to each other in a train. The girl is in the middle. The train goes through a tunnel and it gets completely dark. Suddenly there is a kissing sound and then a sound of a tight slap.

The train comes out of the tunnel. The woman and the Indian look perplexed. The Pakistani is bent over holding his face, all red.

The Pakistani thinks, 'Damn it, that Indian must have tried to kiss the girl, she thought it was me and slapped me.'

The girl thinks, 'That Pakistani must have moved to kiss me and kissed the Indian instead, and got slapped.'

The Indian is thinking, 'If this train goes through another tunnel, I could make another kissing sound and slap that Pakistani again.'

❖

A soldier was having his routine medical check-up. The doctor asked him, 'When did you last do it?'

The soldier replied, '1955.'

The doctor was amazed and asked, 'Why so long ago?'

The soldier glanced at his watch and said, 'But it's only 20:15 now.'

❖

An expectant couple were soon to have their first child. Their doctor told them of a new invention to relieve the mother's pain during childbirth. This invention could be attached to the mother and it would transfer the pain to the baby's father. The couple talked it over and the husband was anxious to help his wife with her delivery. When the blessed time came, they opted to use the new invention. It was strapped to the mother and the dial was set at 1. With the mother's contractions, the husband felt no pain. He asked that the dial be adjusted to 3. With the next contractions, the mother felt less pain and the husband tolerated the experience well. The husband feeling courageous and noble, asked the dial be turned to 10. The nurse did so, and the mother completed the entire labour and delivery with no pain. The husband did not feel any pain either, and was certain that women overrated their plight in childbirth. A few days later the happy new family returned home from the hospital. They were shocked as they drove into their driveway to see the mailman lying dead on the front porch.

❖

When a certain couple went to bed after

watching *Kaun Banega Crorepati* on television, the husband was in an amorous mood. He asked his wife if she wanted to do something about it.

'No,' she said.

'Sure?' he persisted. She nodded in reply.

'Is that your final answer?' he asked.

'Yes,' she said.

'Well then,' the husband said, 'I think I would like to call a friend.

❖

How a man plays the game shows something of his character; how he loses shows all of it.

❖

A young man happened to participate in a competition, which was about writing the shortest story. The organizers' condition was that story ought to have four ingredients—religion, sex, suspense and mystery.

The young man's turn came after many attempts by others. He gave in a story, which was just one sentence long and read: 'Oh God, my wife is going to deliver a child.' Ostensibly amused, the organizers asked the young man whether it contained all the four ingredients. The young man's explanation was as follows: Oh God (religion); My wife (sex); Going to deliver a child (suspense—whether a boy or a girl).

'Okay . . . but where's the mystery?' asked the organizers.

The young man added one more sentence: 'Who is the father?'

The Americans and the Japanese decided to engage in a competitive boat race. Both teams practiced hard and long to reach their peak performance. On the big day the Japanese won by a mile.

The American team was discouraged by the loss. Morale sagged. Corporate management decided that the reason for the crushing defeat had to be found so a consulting firm was hired to investigate the problem and recommend corrective action. The consulting firm's finding was: The Japanese team had eight people rowing and one person steering; the American team had one person rowing and eight people steering.

After a year of study and millions spent analysing the problem, the American team's management structure was completely reorganized. The new structure: four steering managers, three area steering managers and a new performance review system for the person rowing the boat to provide work incentive. The next year, the Japanese won by two miles!

Humiliated, the American corporation laid off the rower for poor performance and gave the managers a bonus for discovering the problem.

❖

A drunk man who smelled like beer sat down on a subway seat next to a priest. The man's tie was stained, his face was plastered with red lipstick, and a half bottle of gin was sticking out of his torn coat pocket. He opened his newspaper and began to read.

After a few minutes the man turned to the priest and asked, 'Say, Father, what causes arthritis?'

'My son, it's caused by loose living, being with cheap, wicked women, too much alcohol and a contempt for the hereafter,' the priest replied.

'You don't say,' the man shook his head sadly.

The priest felt sorry for the poor soul. 'How long have you had arthritis, my son?' he asked gently.

'Oh, I don't have it, Father,' the man replied. 'It says here that the Pope does.'

❖

An elderly man was pushing eighty, but couldn't understand his loss of desire. The doctor was amused. 'Why should it worry you? It's to be expected at your age.'

'But,' pursued the oldster, 'the man next door is eighty-five, and he says he makes love to his wife every night.'

The doctor shrugged, 'Well, can't you say the same thing?'

❖

'Doctor,' said the man on the phone, 'my son has scarlet fever.'

'Yes, I know,' replied the doctor. 'I came by your house and treated him yesterday. Just keep him away from the others in the house and . . .'

'But you don't understand,' said the

distraught parent. 'He's kissed the maid!'

'Well, that's unfortunate. Now we'll probably have to quarantine her . . .'

'And doctor, I'm afraid I've kissed the girl myself.'

'This is getting complicated. That means you may have contracted the disease.'

'Yes, and I've kissed my wife since then.'

'Damn it,' exclaimed the doctor, 'now I'll catch it too!'

❖

There were eleven people hanging on to a rope that came down from a helicopter. Ten were men and one a woman. They all decided that one person should get off because if they didn't, the rope would break and everyone would die. No one could decide who should go, so finally the woman gave a really touching speech saying she would give up her life to save the others, because women were used to giving up things for their husbands and children and giving in to men. When she finished speaking, all the men started clapping . . .

❖

Three female members of an exclusive country club walked into the women's shower room and were shocked to see the lower part of a man's anatomy behind the door of one of the shower stalls.

'Well,' said one of the ladies, 'that certainly isn't my husband.'

The second one added, 'He isn't mine, either.'

And the third, the youngest of the three, said. 'Hell, he isn't even a member of the club.'

❖

What part of the human body,' asked the Anatomy professor, 'is harder than steel?'

Nobody in the class volunteered the information, so he looked in the direction of a sweet co-ed and asked, 'Can you tell me, Miss Riley?'

She blushed a deep scarlet and lowered her eyes, murmuring, 'Oh, please don't ask me to answer that, Professor!'

Crisply, he said, 'The answer is the tissue of the nails. And you, Miss Riley,' he added with a sigh, 'are going to be disappointed.'

❖

A professor attempting to inspire his students says to his class: 'This week is your last chance to study for your final exam scheduled next Monday. Time is running out. The exam is now in the hands of the printer. Are there any questions?'

One student inquires, 'How many questions will there be?'

Another student asks, 'Will the exam

require easy answers?'

A third wants to know, 'Who's the printer?'

❖

Jack and Jill Jerk are sitting in their living room one evening, talking about the future of their young son, George.

'Gee Jack,' says Jill, 'I wonder what little George will grow up to be.'

'I know how we can find out,' says Jack. 'Watch this.' And Jack pulls a ten-dollar bill out of his pocket, setting it on the table. 'If he takes this money,' says Jack smiling, 'then he will grow up to be a banker.' Then Jack takes a dusty old Bible off the bookshelf and sets it on the table next to the money. 'Now,' says Jack excitedly, 'if he takes the Bible, for sure he will grow up to be a great TV evangelist like Jimmy Baker!' Next, Jack pulls out a bottle of whisky from the cabinet and sets it on the table alongside the other items.

'And,' says Jack seriously, 'if he goes for this whisky bottle, then he will just turn out to be a bum!'

Quietly, Jack and Jill Jerk go and hide in the next room when they hear little George coming in. George is whistling happily when he suddenly sees all the articles sitting on the table. He looks around to make sure that he is alone, and then he walks over and picks up the ten-dollar bill. He holds it up to the light and fingers it gently. Then he puts it down, and picks up the Bible. He blows the dust off and thumbs through a few pages, and puts it back down. Little George looks around again, then he quickly uncorks the whisky bottle and sniffs the contents. Suddenly, in one motion he stuffs the money in his pocket, sticks the Bible under his arm, grabs the whisky bottle by the neck and walks out of the room, whistling.

'My goodness,' says Mrs Jerk, 'what does that mean he will grow up to be?'

'Ah!' cries her husband, 'it means he

is going to be a politician.'

❖

Fish for no compliments, they are generally caught in shallow water.

❖

A lady tells her husband to go to the store to buy some cigarettes. He walks down to go to the store only to find it closed. So he goes into a nearby bar to use the vending machine. At the bar he sees a beautiful woman and starts talking to her. They have a couple of beers and one thing leads to another and they end up in her apartment. After they've had their fun, he realizes it is 3 a.m. and says, 'Oh no, it's so late, my wife is going to kill me. Have you got any talcum powder?' She gives him some talcum powder which he proceeds to rub on his hands and then goes home.

His wife is waiting for him in the

doorway and she is pretty angry. 'Where the hell have you been?'

'Well honey, it's like this. I went to the store like you asked me to do, but they were closed. So I went to the bar to use the vending machine. I saw this great looking girl there and we had a few drinks and one thing led to another and I ended up in bed with her.'

'Oh yeah? Let me see your hands!' She sees his hands are covered with powder and . . . 'You god-damn liar! You were gambling again!'

Moral of the story: Always tell yourwife the truth. She won't believe you anyway. At least your conscience is clear.

❖

An eager young man entered his prospective boss's cabin for an interview. Said the boss, 'One thing our company is very particular about is cleanliness. I hope you wiped your shoes on the doormat while coming in?'

Yes, sir,' the young man replied promptly.

Back came the rejoinder, 'One more thing we're very particular about . . . is honesty. There is no doormat outside!'